THE

Philosophy of Literature

BY

CONDÉ B. PALLEN, Ph. D., LL. D.

Omnia per ipsum facta sunt, et sine ipso factum est nihil quod factum est.—St. John, Ev.

Omnia in ipso constant.—St. Paul.

St. Louis, Mo., 1897.
PUBLISHED BY B. HERDER,
17 South Broadway.

801
P166p

PREFACE.

A preface written as an apology is a
superfluity. No man has a right to publish
unless he have a reason for it. If he have
nothing new to say, or if he has not put the
old truth in a new fashion to bring it to fresh
consideration, he has no reason and therefore
no right to utter himself in public. Silence
here is an obligation. But I take it that
where there may be false or foolish speech,
following from great confusion of truth in
men's minds, a true word has paramount
right to be heard. Babel arises from a confusion of truth, and amidst the din of many
voices declaring falsely or purposelessly,
there need be no apology for right utterance.

The word of truth set forth in the following pages I make no claim to be new; it is
an old philosophy; yet in the perennial fullness of its truth ever new. It is the philosophy of literature because it is the philosophy
of all things. Philosophy is the ultimate

word of truth giving the last and sufficient reason for things. My purpose has been to co-ordinate all literary utterance with that final sufficiency. The first principle of truth is the first principle of literature. The philosophy of literature is to be found in the light of that first principle, by which and through which all things are. It is not the philosophy of this day but of all days. It is neither modern nor ancient, because it is eternal. It makes no progress, because is has always been complete. It is independent of human systems of thought, because it transcends them, and, where they are incomplete, perfects them. Where they end it begins; where they terminate in mystery it sheds superabundant light. It is in the philosophy of the Incarnation that we must look for the philosophy of literature. By the light of the Eternal Word made manifest to men in the flesh is human life solved and harmonized. As literature is but a reflex of life, it is only in that same Eternal Word that its meaning may be read aright and its final significance interpreted.

The plan herein followed is simple : in

the first section a statement of the basic
principle of literary utterance, sketched in
large and hasty outline—a loose historical
tracery as it threads the literatures of mankind. The following sections, four in num-
ber, are simply an amplification of this
thesis, not by any historical method, but by
way of a philosophical analysis and synthesis
of the primary principles laid down in the
first section.

The lecture form in which the five papers
or sections were composed, I have retained;
as I conceive that the reader may, without
violence to the proprieties, be regarded at the
same time as auditor.

CONDÉ B. PALLEN.

St. Louis, December, 1896.

CONTENTS.

THESIS:

THE CATHOLICITY OF LITERATURE.

Contents.

Contents.

SCIENCE:

THEOLOGY, THE LIGHT OF LITERATURE.

x *Contents.*

Contents.

SYNTHESIS.

Contents. XV

STYLE :

THE VARIETY OF THE FREEDOM OF THE WORD.

Contents.

THESIS:

THE

CATHOLICITY OF LITERATURE.

———•———

Literature is the written expression of man's various relations to the universe and its Creator. The foundations of all things lie hidden in the Divine Essence, and for man, "the roof and crown of things," were all things made, and he, fashioned in the image of his Maker, for God. Man's life therefore can only be adequately measured by the end for which he was created. His manifold relations to the universe, to his fellow men and to himself, are seen truly and distinctly only in his relations to God. This is why, in all great questions, be they political, social, religious, literary or scientific, a great question of theology is involved. "Theology," says Donoso Cortes, "inasmuch as it is the science of God, is the ocean which contains and embraces all sciences, as God is the ocean

which contains and embraces all things."
In this do we discover the reason of the Catholicity of all truth, and in this the reason
why the utterance of all true things is Catholic. It was this that led St. Justin, martyr,
to say, "Whatsoever things have been truly
said by mankind, properly belong to us
Christians." For all true human utterance
is one in the indivisible unity of truth, and
so we claim for all true literature Catholicity
as its distinctive note. It is this Catholicity
of literature that furnishes us with the universal ground of our inquiry into its philosophy.

Since, therefore, man's life lies within
the Divine embrace, and his literature is the
reflection of his life, in that literature we shall
find the Divine reflex mirrored, broken and
distorted it is true, except in the Catholic
word, but nevertheless the one element which
gives human life its tone and color, its form
and its beauty, its interest and its truth, and
without which even its tragedy were meaningless. A non-Catholic writer gives utterance to a great Catholic truth when he
says, "The grand relation of man is not first

to his brother man, but to something else, that is beyond humanity—that is at once without and also beyond himself ; to this first, and to his brother man through this. We are not our own ; we are bought with a price. Our bodies are God's temples, and the joy and terror of life depends on our keeping these temples pure, or defiling them. Such are the solemn and profound beliefs, whether conscious or unconscious, on which all the higher art of the world has based itself. All the profundity and solemnity of it is borrowed from these and exists for us in exact proportion to the intensity with which we hold them.''

This primal relation to God is the basis of literature, and even when men seem furthest away from God, none the less distinctly but more darkly and awfully does the shadow of this dependence grow. Let us glance for a moment at the literatures of the ancient world, where that shadow hung in its deepest intensity.

Dating back to the prehistoric era of the Aryan race we find the Vedas the most ancient monument of human literature among

our own ancestors. It was the Aryan book
of revelations, their sacred writings in which
was contained for them the divine word,
whence was drawn the rule and guide
of their life, and whence blossomed, as
the flower from the branch, their voluminous writings. It treats of man's relation to
God, or rather to the gods into which their
darkened imagination had divided the divine
unity, for they, like fallen man elsewhere
throughout the ancient world, had strayed
away from the primal light and groped dimly
in the shadow of their sins. But the
essence and doctrine of the Vedas, dark and
grotesque as it often was, taught the necessary and indispensable truth that man's first
relation was to a Divine Being, and that
out of this grew all other relations to his
fellow men. Having confounded God with
His creation, the Aryan mind had degenerated
to a nature-worship, out of which grew its
vast mythological system. The two great
Indian epics, the Ramayana and Mahabharata, breathe the same religious instinct and
inculcate the same doctrine. One is the
history of the incarnation of the God Vishnu,

who comes to rescue the people from a demon
prince, and the other, the Mahabharata,
relates the struggle for mastery between two
contending dynasties. Each is essentially
religious in its character, and is interwoven
with the teachings of Brahmanism. It is the
religious element in them that gives them
their substance. Without the religious light
they would lose their color and their meaning. The eternal right and wrong of things,
founded in the Divine nature, is the pivot of
all their interest. Throughout all Hindoo
literature we find the religious element char-
acteristically prevailing. Buddhist literature feeds ever upon the same notion, but its
shadows are deeper and stronger on account
of its terrible doctrine of the essential evil of
living. The Tripitaka, the sacred book of
the Buddhists, is devoted to the elucidation
of the doctrine how men by right living in
conformity with divine things, may escape
the evil of existence and enter into Nirvana,
the eternal cessation of finite existence.

In the Avesta, the sacred book of the
Persians, the only remaining monument of a
once extensive literature, is described the

conflict between the powers of light and
darkness, the principles of good and evil, and
how men must conform with the law of
Ormuzd, the Supreme Good, if they hope to
ever attain holiness and enter upon eternal
life. In the Assyrio-Chaldaic writings we
find the same religious tone prevailing; all
was from the gods and through the gods. The
well-being of man consisted in his doing the
divine will; therein lay virtue and happiness.
The idea that man lived perpetually under
the supervision of the gods, to whom he
owed all, and to whom he must render an
account of all, was ever present to the
Assyrian mind. "O my Lord," runs a
penitential psalm, "My sins are many, my
trespasses are great; and the wrath of the
gods hath plagued me with disease, and with
sickness and sorrow. O Lord, do not abandon
thy servant. In the waters of the great
storm seize his hand. The sins which he
has committed turn thou to righteousness."

How thoroughly saturated was Egyptian
life with the religious idea is made evident
at every turn in that strange land by the
inscriptions on their monuments and tombs.

The life after death lay like a nightmare upon the Egyptian mind. In the land of the Amenti, the regions of the dead, the soul stood in the presence of its judge, Osiris, to render an account of its earthly pilgrimage. To be able to pass that scathing ordeal was the controlling motive of the son of Mizraim. The book of the Dead, containing the account of the funeral ritual and the trial of the soul before the tribunal of Osiris, may be called the sacred scriptures of the Egyptians, and like all the sacred writings of the ancient world, the greatest monument of their literature as well as its source.

But there is one ancient people among whom this law of literature failed to find expression. The Chinese early in their history fell under the blight of Confucianism, and are to-day what they were three thousand years ago, a living exemplification of the sterility of Agnosticism. Confucianism failed to recognize the divine source of human life. Confucius, like the modern Agnostics, refused to acknowledge God or a future life. He taught that the Supreme Being was an uknowable God, and based his ethics upon

man's relations to man alone. Under this
direful influence the Chinese and their literature became inmovably stereotyped. They
stagnated in a sterile formalism, and their
civilization became mummified. Their very
language congealed into monosyllables. The
sap of spiritual life has perished amongst
them, and they stand to-day the living witnesses of that death which ever falls upon a
people who have lost faith in divine things.

When we turn to the Greeks, whose
literary art has wielded such a potent external influence over our own, we find the
religious element permeating every page of
their great literary productions. What were
the Iliad and the Odyssey without the gods?
There, as distinctly as anywhere in ancient
pagan literature, does the human dependence
upon the divine—however fantastically conceived—that primal relationship of man to
something beyond himself, stand out distinctly as the ground of human action, the
underlying basis of human existence. Homer
was the fountain head of Greek literature,
the source of its prolific inspiration, the
master model of its genius. Its greatest

dramatists, Æschylus and Sophocles built up
their great tragedies on this same conception,
the divine foundation which upheld the life
of man. Without the sense of that grand
relation of man to something beyond mun-
dane humanity, what value or meaning
attaches to Prometheus Bound or Œdipus
Rex? Among the Greek philosophers, who
stands pre-eminent in that great galaxy?
Pythagoras, Socrates, Plato and Aristotle,
with whom the divine was the beginning and
the end. Sceptic, Cynic and Stoic, who
denied or doubted the divine, and are only
known by value of their negation, play but
a secondary and ignoble part, and that, in
the decadency of the Greek intellect.

As with Greece so was it with Rome.
Without Capitoline Jove Rome was nothing.
From Numa came her ancient wisdom, and it
was believed that he had received it directly
from heaven. Her life grew out of the religious element and she moved to the conquest
of the world under the domination of the
idea that she was divinely fated to the dominion of the world, and indeed, under the
guiding hand of a Providence, unseen by her,

she was secretly led to the fulfilment of a
design more stupendous than ever the mind
of man had grasped. Her literature is
largely concerned with divine things, or else
supposes her politico-religious genius as the
animating principle of her existence. The
constant theme of her poets is the gods and
their intercourse with men. Her prose
writers discuss the nature of the divinities
and Roman virtue founded in religion, and
insist upon the recognition of the divine in
the Roman state as the basis of Rome's
stability. The Æneid is simply the divine
genealogy of the Roman people. Æneas was
the son of a goddess; Romulus was equally of
divine origin, so radical in the Roman mind
was this conception of the necessary relation of
the Roman people to the divine. Strike this
notion out of Roman life, and you destroy
the root of her greatness. Rome without
Capitoline Jove would never have been Rome,
and her literary expression would never have
burgeoned without the animus of that
thought.

Thus, throughout the whole pagan
world, with one signal exception, do we find

the recognition of something beyond humanity. It becomes the vivifying principle of their existence and the substance of their literature. It is the broken and distorted image of God mirrored in the life of pagan man. Night had closed in upon his mind, and the Divine Image was reflected from his darkened imagination brokenly and grotesquely. With his faculties impaired by sin, his reason clouded, his will weakened, and his passions inflamed, pagan man had lost sight of the divine beauty of his Creator. The image of sin had obscured the primal light, and the Divine Presence overshadowed the world in the clouds of a divine wrath. Men knew not God in that pristine beauty in which he had first revealed Himself to them, but the justice of His outraged majesty had fallen upon them, and the weight of their sin burdened them like a leaden garment. It was the universal sense of the ancient world that man had fallen from a first high estate through sin, that the harmony of human existence had been broken by rebellion against the Divine Decree. Return to the divine order was imperative, and it

was clearly recognized that sacrifice and
penalty were the roads to reconciliation.
Hence that overwhelming sense everywhere
present, that man's first relation was to the
divine, and through it to his fellow-man.
This it was that lay at the basis of his
life, and this was the soil out of which
sprang his literature. Do away with this,
and you destroy at one fell stroke its
underlying motif. It was this pointing back-
wards to a lost estate and the overwhelming
sense of a radical loss that gave interest and
zest to human existence. There would not
have shone even the lurid glare of man's
disordered passion save for the presence of
that first divine light reflected through the
chaos of sin. Man, by his rebellion
against heaven, had broken with the divine order; to that order he felt himself
primarily bound, and from that obligation
were all the duties of his existence derived.

But there was one people of the ancient world, who yet lived in the Divine
Presence, and dwelt in the light of the
first revelation. They recognized, distinctly
and fully, what the pagan world dimly

and confusedly felt. With them the ancient
light had never gone out, and they bore it
through the ages intact until the fulfilment
of that time, when the great Reconcilement
was accomplished. The ancient Jews knew
God. That grand relation of man to something beyond humanity was to the Chosen
People the visible inspiration of their lives.
They had not confounded God with His own
creation : He was Jehovah who had made
man " to His own image and likeness," and
who had promised to redeem him. Through
Moses and His prophets had He spoken to
them and delivered His law. Theirs was an
immediate relation to God, and so intense
was this faith in their direct relationship to
God that it became the very pith and marrow
of their social and political existence. The
pagan world had lost sight of the One
Supreme Divine Being, the Creator, Sus-
tainer and Governor of the universe, and
had rendered divine homage to false gods.
But to the Jew, Jehovah was first and alone,
the one and the only God. This conception
is the key-note of Hebrew literature, and no
ancient literature is comparable to it. The

polish of Greek and Roman classics grows
flaccid in presence of the magnificent simplicity and the awful sublimity of the Old
Testament. Nowhere in the whole range of
the world's literature do we find anything
approaching it in those two primary qualities
of all great art—simplicity and sublimity.
Nor is this to be wondered at when we
remember that the greatest art is ever based
upon the recognition that man's first and
highest relation is to God and through God
to his fellow-men. This is the vivifying
principle of the Old Testament in the
intensest manner, and in proportion to
the intensity with which this conception
is there realized, do these qualities of simplicity and sublimity shine forth. It
strikes the gamut of all literary art ; it is
history, it is epic ; its lyric qualities are
unsurpassed, from the exquisite domestic idyl
of Ruth to the supreme height of the Canticle
of Canticles ; its didactic poetry is unequaled
in Proverbs and Ecclesiastes ; the book of Job
soars supremely, and the Lamentations of
Jeremiah are beyond compare the foremost
elegy of all time. It is indeed the Book

of Books, for it is the divine presence in the human heart singing the Canticle of the Universe.

With the first chapter of Genesis begins the Catholicity of Literature in the first divinely spoken word : "In the beginning God created the heavens and the earth." And this is supplemented and completed in the mysteriously sublime and sublimely mysterious Gospel of St. John ; "In the beginning was the Word, and the Word was with God, and the Word was God." The Old Testament was the divine prelude to the New, as the old Law was the promise of the new. No wonder the song was sublime whose theme was the prophecy of the coming of the Son of God. "And the Word was made flesh and dwelt among us ; " and the great prophecy was fulfilled, and the great song closed in that divinest of all harmonies—God become man. "In Him was Life, and the Life was the light of men : and the light shineth in darkness, and the darkness did not comprehend it." The ancient world lay in the shadows of the valley of death. The darkness of sin had enwrapt the mind of man, and he wandered helplessly through the night. The glory of Rome was but the lurid glare of pride, and her greatness was but the lust of dominion. The subtle Greek intellect could shed no light upon that darkness, and her genius served only to lighten up its profundity. Man, like Prometheus bound, lay prostrate in the bonds of his own ignorance, for he had lost sight of the first principle of all knowledge, the knowledge of God. "And the light shineth in darkness, and the darkness did not comprehend it. He was in the world, and the world was made by Him, and the world knew Him not. He came unto His own, and His own received Him not." The desire of the prophets and the expected of the nations had, in the fullness of time, come to accomplish the great reconciliation and lead men from the darkness to the light. A new principle had entered into the life of the world, for human nature, assumed by the Divine Person of our Lord Jesus Christ, had been made over anew, and the Father was revealed to Man as He is known to the Son.

The Incarnation of the Son of God is the pivot of the world's history. It is the central fact of all time, it is the first and last fact in the history of mankind. From it are all things; to it are all things; by it are all things; it is the measure and the sum of humanity; it is the supreme moment of time, the center of all space! It was in time, and yet from and for eternity; it knows no measure but itself, no reason greater than itself; it is beyond man, and yet for man; it is by God, and yet by man; it is the Alpha and Omega of all things; it is the one and sole Word which explains the universe of things. The ancient world is meaningless except in its prospect; and the modern world is an enigma save for the light that it sheds upon it. When the Divine Word became Man, the old world in the glory of the Roman state, had reached the zenith of its greatness, and at the same time sounded the abyss of its degradation. Henceforth that greatness became her weakness, and she was to serve as the human means in the hands of Divine Power for the establishment of a dominion more universal than her own, and with a life that will outlive her own by the length of all the ages. The Greek mind had elaborated

a philosophy, which had reached the limits of
human reason ; henceforth, that philosophy
was to be the handmaiden of the Truth,
which had come into the world in the person
of our Lord and Saviour. He had truly come
in the fullness of time ; the ancient order
had reached its culmination, for man had
arrived at the limits of his wanderings in the
valley of death ; henceforth, he is to live in
the presence of that life which is the Light
of men ; man's life now assumes a new
aspect and a new relation, for "the only
begotten Son, who is in the bosom of the
Father, he hath declared Him."

As all things in the ancient order focused
towards that great central fact, so, in the
modern, all things radiate from it. A new
order of life is established, for that grand
primal relation of man to God is re-established
and perfected. The pagan world had not
known God, and had destroyed the simplicity
of His divinity; the Jews had known God but
not in His fullness; but Jesus Christ knows
the Father, and has declared Him to us.
Besides this fuller revelation of the Father,
there is this additional manifestation : "The

Word was made flesh and dwelt among us ; "
God has become man ; has assumed human
nature and united it with His divinity,
regenerated man and lifted him from the
sloughs of sin to the heights of grace. Man
now not only knows God as the Jews did, but
he knows God in the flesh—God as man with
this same human nature of ours redeemed
from the bondage of sin and made co-heir of
heaven with the Son of God who is our
Brother.

Out of this great event, the most
momentous in the life of humanity, sprang a
new life to the world, and from this new life
a new literature. First, we have the history
of our Lord Jesus Christ Himself by the four
Evangelists, and as never was or will be a life
like His, so never was or will be a history
like theirs. As the Old Testament is to the
ancient, so is the New Testament to the modern world. It is unique and sublime beyond
compare. Its simplicity and sublimity excel
all the written words of men. As a supplement to this wonderful biography come the
Acts of the Apostles and the Epistles, centered
and clustered around that great fact of the

Incarnation. Then followed the period of the Greek and Latin Fathers. Its literature was builded out of the same tremendous fact, the Incarnation ; it is an edifice built forever by the master hands of Ignatius, Justin Martyr, Polycarp, Irenæus, Tertullian, Origen, Clement, Cyprian, Athanasius, Ambrose, Chrysostom, and as the roof and crown of that magnificent intellectual temple to the glory of the Word made flesh, the great St. Augustine. The exposition of the great truth of the Incarnation and all the great truths that flowed from it was the one theme of Patristic literature. "The Word made flesh " was its central idea ; the divinity of our Lord Jesus Christ was its one inspiration. It expounded and defended the integrity of the Divine Human Nature. "And the light shineth in darkness, and the darkness did not comprehend it." The pagan world, blinded by its own sin, refused to acknowledge Him. Heresy after heresy arose to assail the integrity of His Divine Human Nature. Human pride and human passion assaulted again and again the citadel of Faith. Now the Divinity of our Lord was denied and now

His Humanity, and the great fathers, both in the written and in the oral word, defended the Divine Word made flesh, and for all time laid the foundations of this Divine truth deep and broad, firm and impregnable.

St. Augustine closed that great era. He was the diapason of that splendid chorus attesting to the light of the Eternal Word amongst men and the doctrine of our Lord's Divine human nature. He lived in an age which witnessed the dissolution of Rome. He saw that ship of state, which Horace had so pleadingly apostrophized in the palmy days of Augustus, a helpless wreck upon the cruel rocks with the floods of destruction pouring over her. Amidst the stress of the storm, when the enemies of the Faith had charged the Christians with the authorship of the calamities overwhelming Rome through the wrath of the gods, he did what had never been done before, wrote a philosophy of history in defense of himself and his fellow-Catholics. The pagan world had never produced a philosophy of history, and never could have, for it was never able to rise to the conception of the solidarity of the human

race or the Christian notion of a Divine Providence moulding and controlling human
events to its own ends, and yet without
disturbing the freedom of human action.
The heathen world knew only Fate, and
forgot freedom, because it had forgotten God.
It saw only misfortune where Christianity
recognized penalty; it groaned beneath the
burden of that misfortune, where Christianity
rejoiced in the purifying action of penalty ;
it saw only avenging deities, where Christianity recognized the justice of God in the
punishment of sin, and the divine mercy in
the expiatory virtue of suffering ; it knew no
method of reconcilement, because it had lost
sight of the divine love, whilst Christianity
was that very means of redemption, the
bridge of grace and the bond of love by which
man is again united to his Maker. No philosophy of history was possible until Christianity had impregnated the mind of man
with these higher conceptions of his own
destiny, and taught him to look upon men in
the unity of Christ redeeming the world from
the universal bondage of sin. For four
centuries had this Christian thought leavened

the mind of the Roman world; for four
centuries had it been expounded, dwelt upon,
developed and defended by the Greek and
Latin Fathers, until at length, the times were
ripe for the great conception of St. Augustine,
and on those foundations, whose center of
gravity was the doctrine of the Incarnation,
rose that Titanic structure, the last, the
greatest and the truest work of Roman genius,
the City of God. "As to what concerns
history," says a French writer, "the following is the idea of St. Augustine. The events
of this world are neither fortuitous nor
isolated. Divine Providence directs them,
forms them into a series, causes them all
to concur to the same end, the triumph
of truth and justice, such as they were
revealed in the first instance to the Hebrew
people, and as Jesus Christ came to confirm
and announce them to the nations. Who-
ever listens to the voice from on high, and
follows it, belongs to the people of the elect,
the City of God, nigh to which moves the
city of the earth, devoted to wordly interests,
the city of pride and dominion, the perse-
cutor of the saints, but which not the less

labors, by means of which she is ignorant,
for the kingdom of God. Thus did Baby-
lon in the east,—thus does Rome in the
west—both of them queens of nations, both
of them announced by prophecies, both of
them predestined to spread abroad, the
former, the revelations of the Old Testament, the latter, those of the New. The
kingdom of Rome was universal, because
such was the Kingdom of Christ. And as
the ancient law was but a preparation for
the new, everything in the ancient world
converged towards Rome, and the accession
of Jesus Christ, just as everything after
that accession has concurred to the triumph
and universality of the Christian Faith. . . ."

After the death of St. Augustine followed a lull in the activity of the intellectual life of the world. Rome had passed
into death. After a reign of twelve hundred
years, Rome became the spoil of robber
hordes. Goth and Visigoth, Hun and
Vandal poured down upon the broken
empire like swarms of devastating locusts,
and devoured it. For the next four centuries all was turmoil and confusion. A

new people had supplanted the old, and the
barbaric blood of the north took possession
of the ruined empire. The barbarians were
fresh, vigorous, untamed and uncouth. It
took time to subdue them to the stability of a
settled life. These four centuries were a
period of parturition ; society was in the
travail of the birth of new nations. In the
midst of such confusion and instability there
was little time for thought or reflection ; it
was a time of action, and the immaturity of
the barbarian mind with the unceasing
demand made upon man's energies in building up the social and political structure of
new nations in these distressing ages, was
scarcely compatible with the development
of literature. These ages are called dark, but
they were dark only because the time had
not come for the light ; they were dark
because no light comes to the child in the
womb.

Towards the end of the eighth century
the new dawn appears in the reign of the great
Charlemagne. Something like security and
peace had settled upon Europe, and then
began the renaissance, for from this time

dates the real re-birth of letters. Simultaneous
with the birth of the Gothic Cathedral, the
fitting expression of the mediæval mind,
came about that second great intellectual
movement in the world of Catholic literature,
the building up of scholastic philosophy,
that superb demonstration of the harmony
between reason and faith. The Fathers had
laid the divine premises ; they had elaborated
and developed the theological side of revealed
truth. With them it was not a question of
the relation of the supernatural to the
natural, of revealed truth to natural truth.
They quarried that stupendous temple of
theological science out of the inexhaustible
rock of the doctrine of the Incarnation, nor
did they seek for other material beyond.
But scholastic philosophy in the divine light
of their labors constructed its great edifice,
its Gothic Cathedral, from human materials ;
laid its foundations deep in the earth, and
lifted its tapering spires till they glinted in
the light of heaven itself. Even as in those
ages of faith one generation began the
foundations of those great cathedrals, that
stand to-day as everlasting monuments of

human skill divinely inspired, and a third and a fourth generation completed the work, so did the master hands of scholastic philosophers from generation to generation labor through the centuries in the building up of that great system of human reason which has established in the intellectual order the reconcilement of human with divine things.

Nor could this have been accomplished until the Divine Science had been formulated on the one hand and the rational science had been elaborated on the other. The age of patristic literature furnished the first, and the Greek philosophers, the keenest intellects of the ancient world, had constructed the other. Nor could this adjustment have been brought about until the mind of man had been moulded to the truth of Christianity, for not until then were the necessary means of such a reconcilement perceived by him. The ancient world dimly and confusedly recognized the disorder in human nature, but it never conceived nor could have ever understood the scheme of redemption. So in the intellectual order it was aware of the defects and limitations of human reason, but it saw no way of healing the hurt or restoring the truth. This task in the order of divine providence was the work of the scholastic period. The first four centuries of Christianity saw the development of theological science ; the second four centuries saw the political fabric of Rome sink into dust, and the building up of a new social sructure on Catholic lines out of the fresh material, which the barbarians had contributed to the Christian cause ; the third four, from the eighth to the twelfth century, witnessed the intellectual adjustment between faith and reason, the harmonious combination of the divine science of the fathers with the human science of the Greek philosophers, the reconcilement of the science of St. Ignatius and Augustine with the science of Socrates and Aristotle. As St. Augustine was the completion of the Patristic era, so was St. Thomas the culmination of the scholastic period. He is the prince of theologians, as well as the prince of philosophers. Summed up in him is the full-flowered genius of scholasticism, and he remains to-day, pre-eminent among all, the

master theologian, and the master philoso-
pher. So deep, so broad, so profound, so
elevated is the science of the Angel of the
Schools, that he has come to be universally
recognized as *the* Doctor of the Church.
Popes and Councils have extolled his genius,
and the homage of the entire Catholic intellectual world is a perpetual monument to his
saintly greatness. In his great Summæ, the
two orders of truth, two through the limitations only of the human mind, become the
one consonant, harmonious whole of truth
flowing from the everlasting bosom of God.
In his hands human reason becomes con-
sistent ; it reaches the limits of its power,
and flowers into the full dignity of its nature,
neither debased by skeptical contradictions,
nor inflated by an impious pride. It is
man's highest faculty by which he is specif-
ically distinguished from the brute creation,
and whereby elevated by grace he arrives at
his greatest perfection in the contemplation
of truth.

With St. Thomas the scholastic movement, properly speaking, culminated. The
foundations of revealed and natural truth had

been laid, and an era of a development of
another character set in.   As a link between
the period just passed and the coming era,
Dante's great song, like a sublime anthem,
connecting earth with heaven, fittingly closes
the one and ushers in the other, and embodies
the main characteristics of both,   It is scholastic philosophy in poetic form; it is human
reason poured into the alembic of a fervid
and magnificent imagination, and the divine
science of theology winged with a fancy
soaring to the empyrean itself.   The soul of
man never before nor after dared such a flight
as Dante's, and none but a Catholic soul,
which had breathed the atmosphere of St.
Thomas, could have sounded the profundity
of hell and winged its way through the crystalline spheres of heaven.   The science of
Aristotle and the science of St. Thomas
blended with the most consummate art, an art
flowering from the deep soil of Catholic truth,
are united in the organ-like harmony of the
Divina Commedia.   Reason, faith and art lift
their voices in a sublime chorus to the divine
source of all, till the heavens and the earth
tremble with the holy canticle.   Worthy

companions, the Divina Commedia and the great Summæ of St. Thomas, and each the supremest effort of the human mind in science and in art.

While the great foundations were being laid in the intellectual world, the social and national life of Europe was being formed. By the time of Dante's death the great nations had crystallized into their distinctive factors, and during the two centuries following, gradually settled, through the slow dissolution of the feudal system into a stable political form. The nomadic instinct of the barbarian had been subdued, and yielded in the main, to the yoke of law. During these centuries, the fourteenth and fifteenth, the artistic life of Europe was fast developing to its maturity. The beauty of Christian truth was beginning to shine in upon men's souls, until at last the sun of Christian art burst in full splendor upon the world, in the genius of Michael Angelo and Raphael. With this development came the cultivation of the Belles-lettres, which now found a congenial soil whence to draw sustenance, for, not until scholasticism had ploughed the land and

made it rich with the vigor of its profound
science, could the seeds of fine art have a
fitting place to strike root. From this soil
burgeoned the great literatures of Spain,
France and England in the sixteenth century.
After the sixteenth century, when the sterile
influence of the unartistic Reformation began
to be more widely and potently felt, the
decline followed.

The period now set in was pre-eminently
the artistic in its character. It arose only
after the truth of the divine and intellectual
order had been thoroughly established and
settled by scholastic philosophy. Men had
conceived and realized the truth of things as
scholasticism had expounded to them the
order of the universe and man's relations to
God. The literature of this new era was
built upon these accepted truths, and drew
its great inspiration from these perennial
wells of Catholic science. The soil had been
well prepared, and art burgeoned from it in a
splendid luxuriance. In our own tongue, out
of that same field, grew the genius of Shake-
speare and the Elizabethan dramatists ; for,
although England had seceded from the

Holy See, its Protestantism had not yet penetrated to the hearts of its people and the Elizabethan literature was too great and too far-reaching to have been affected by the barren negation of the Reformation.

Unfortunately this continuity of development was fatally interrupted by the religious rebellion of the sixteenth century. The rich stream of truth, that had so abundantly fertilized the soil of Christendom, was diverted from its onward flow and disastrously dammed up by Luther's denial of the unity of truth. Theological and philosophical truth suffered a rude violence, and division and discord usurped the place of unity and amity. The development of great Christian literature has been retarded ever since. In the greater and sublimer qualities, Christian literature has never risen again to the height to which it then soared when the unity of truth gave it wings. There has been literature in the succeeding centuries, but never since have the great constellations of that period been equaled in depth and brilliancy. And in proportion as the negation and doubt sprung from

Luther's denial, have reached down into the lives of the people, so has modern literature dwindled and lessened, though indeed, there has been much literature and here and there great authors who have transcended the narrow limitations of their circumstances. The effect in the world of literature has been slow but sure, until to-day we are reaping its final and baleful results in the complete denial of that something beyond humanity, upon whose belief the great art-work of the world has always depended, and in a species of art and literature, that has turned from God and abandoned man to a bestial realism.

Let us trace the destructive expansion of this principle of negation down to our own times.

Luther started upon the principle of the denial of the authority of truth, and therefore, of the unity of truth. It was the assertion in the religious order of that principle of desintegration, which in the social and political orders culminates in anarchy—Individualism, or the assumption that every man is a sufficient law unto himself. This is the basis of the principle of private interpretation. Henceforth man's religious creed is not proposed to his belief from a source outside of him, but he makes his creed out of his own inner consciousness. Religion, therefore, becomes subjectivism, and man is no longer dependent upon God, but God upon man. This is, of course, the direct reversal of the Catholic order. As men always seek to give their religious beliefs a rational basis, to vindicate their faith at the bar of reason, hand-in-hand with this religious subjectivism has developed a sympathetic philosophic movement. Protestantism at once began to seek a subjective basis for itself in the order of natural truth. Des Cartes was the father of the fatal method, and Protestant Germany completed the work he had so rashly begun. Kant elaborated his doctrine of phenomena, wherein the objective reality of the world was denied and Fichte, Schelling and Hegel were his logical children. In their hands, the entire universe has at last evaporated into the vague absolute of Transcendentalism. In Holland, out of this same skepticism, Spinoza

begot his pantheism, and in England Locke
and Hume were the progenitors of Spencer.
The conclusion of all this modern philosophic
parturition is agnosticism, in which God is
nothing and man is everything; and the
rational basis upon which Protestantism has
endeavored to place its creed has been the
source of its destruction. The religious
denial of the sixteenth century has ended in
the agnostic denial of the nineteenth. Like
begets like, and one contradiction begets
another. The first falsehood has begot a
second, and each is self-destructive. The
Reformation denied the Church, and agnosticism has denied the Reformation, and with
it God.

This process of philosophical development, or rather degradation, has made a deep
impress upon modern literature. In the
eighteenth century, it produced the shallow
cynicism of Voltaire and the gigantic small-
ness of the Encyclopædists. Theirs was the
literature of the sneer and the scoff. It was
considered sufficient to subject religion to the
obloquy of words to confute all claims of the
supernatural. "Priestcraft" was the sole

explanation of the religious sentiment of
mankind, and when the Voltaireans had
hurled that obnoxious epithet, they concluded
that the battle was ended. But the eighteenth
century with its mocking skepticism has lived
itself out, and subjectivism has developed a
far more formidable phase, as it has advanced
nearer to its final term. Its negation has
grown broader and deeper, until the poison
has now eaten under the very foundations of
human faith in the supernatural. The
currents of the movement have set in with
full force, and are fed from two great sources.
In the first place Protestantism has lost its
hold as a binding creed upon the mass of its
adherents. Faith is no longer exacted, and
those who profess may believe what part they
please, or reject the whole. What is still left
is a Humanitarianism, which has found its
specific expression in the doctrines of Positiv-
ism. Individualism, or the right of private
interpretation, has finally so decimated the
sects that there is nothing now left of them
save a vague shadow in print, spelt with a
capital letter. On this there is an emphatic
consensus of opinion, because it involves

nothing definite or binding. In other words, Individualism has denied all that is positive in religion, and so sapped the very foundations of belief. It believes nothing, and yet would leave men free to believe anything.

The second element, which has contributed largely to this denial of the supernatural has been the enormous development, which physical science has made in the last half-century. Physical science has at last resolved the whole universe into matter and force. It sees nothing personal in these final elements; it recognizes nothing but an unconscious energy working blindly and inexorably, whither, it cannot in modesty pretend to say. In this view man is simply materially co-ordinated with the blind energy at the back of the universe, this Unknowable What. Human nature, therefore, at once sinks to a level in kind with all other natural phenomena, and men are only a finer clay than the brutes.

Thus has Individualism devoured itself, and with the assistance of physical science destroyed the individual by making him a fleeting particle of world force. The supreme individual has now lapsed into supreme force, and man's personality, having lost all relation to the supernatural, that something which is at once without, and beyond himself, is submerged in the pantheistic seas of the unknowable. Subjectivism, in trying to find a rational basis for the individual in himself, has destroyed him, swallowed him helplessly in the cataclysm of his own nonentity. Human personality is denied, and therefore human freedom, because man's relation to the supernatural has been denied. In the political world the result is socialism, in the religious pantheism, and in the philosophical world the pessimism of Schoepenhaur and Von Hartman, and in the practical world,—suicide.

Thus the modern movement, the subjectivism developing out of the negation of the sixteenth century, has culminated in the absolute denial of man's relation to that which is at the same time without and beyond himself.

It is the realization of this grand primal relation to God that makes the basis of all the great art-work of the world. We saw how the literary genius of the ancient world,

after its own fashion, drew its inspiration
and its life from it, and we notice the one
memorable exception in Confucianism and
the consequent sterility amongst the Chinese.
We saw how this was the very heart's core
of the Old Testament, the greatest literature
of the ancient world, and we trace in
Christianity the confirmation and the completion of this conception. Patristic literature
laid the supernatural premises and developed
the divine science; Scholasticism established
the harmony between this divine science and
human reason. After the foundations of
truth had thus been laid, we saw how the
sublime edifice of Christian art was built
upon them.

With the great denial came the beginning of the end of all that had gone before,
and to-day we see its fatal subjectivism fully
developed, sweeping like an angry tide
against those eternal foundations. From
such a source can spring no art. What
tragedy or comedy can there be in an aggre-
gation of atoms? What responsibility or
freedom is there in a molecule? Can there
be any moral relation between a man's brain

and the blind energy of a scientific universe ? Thought, we have been told by modern subjectivists, is but the breaking up and remarshalling of the atoms of the brain. What meaning can be attached to the words right and wrong in presence of this fatal mechanism ? We are not bought with a price, our bodies are not God's temples, but bundles of nervous ganglia in which works the blind unconscious force of matter. The joy and terror of life do not depend upon our keeping these temples pure or defiling them, for molecular motion knows no difference between the pure and the foul, between holiness and wickedness. Man neither knows, nor can know, anything beyond himself, and he stands only as the momentary equilibrium of nature's blind energies working in and through the tissues of his evanescent frame.

As a matter of fact, subjectivism has produced no literature except that of denial, and its value lies not in any positive truth inculcated, but in the truth denied. It has never declared a new truth, and its interest lies only in its negation of the old. What artistic merit it possesses arises from the reflection of the truth it would destroy ; it inversely awakens our sympathies only because it seeks to sever them from the source which has developed them, and negatively appeals to our æsthetic taste only in so far as it denies that sense of the beautiful which Christianity has implanted in our hearts. If the Catholic view of life— that view which regards men's bodies as God's temples to be kept pure and undefiled —were suddenly eliminated from our conception of life, what value would the subjective denial have, or what interest would be still retained in its destructive processes ?

In all the literature which has come under the influence of the subjective movement, point out any one instance of literary art, whose interest does not center around its doctrine of denial, or else in the assumption of the Christian ideal of life.

It is in the modern novel that we see this best illustrated, for there we find modern life most universally and accurately reflected, and this is the characteristic form which modern literary art has generally taken. What is the general character of this literature, and on what does its interest hinge? Modern fiction may be ranged under three general heads, the religious novel, the scientific novel and the realistic novel. The religious novel deals directly with this question of man's relation to the supernatural; this is its professed theme, the motive of its action and the center of its interest. What dramatic or artistic quality would there be in *Robert Elsmere*, except for the torture of soul which that sensitive clergyman endures in the struggle between his faith and his reason? Its tragedy lies precisely in his abandonment of that faith in the supernatural which has formed the basis of his life. It interests us only because we feel that he has felt the supreme value of the faith he has lost and the void it has made in his life, and this in spite of the author's attempt at compensation by turning him into an enthusiastic humanitarian. When the hero has finally renounced his belief in Christianity, the dramatic action of the book ceases, its interest wanes and it sinks to the commonplace. Robert Elsmere is one of its class and perhaps the best representative of

its type, and in it we have the necessity
which forces subjective literature, that is,
the literature which denies the supernatural
to find a theme in that relation of man to
the supernatural, even though it be to sever
that divine bond.

The scientific novel treats of the same
subject, but approaches it in another way.
It groups its interest around the attitude
which modern science has assumed towards
the supernatural. It discusses the purely
materialistic denial of religion and its results
in practical life. It pictures the outcome of
molecular ethics as the basis of human
action. In *Dr. Rameau*, by George Ohnet,
we have a picture of science, in the person
of a learned doctor, yielding finally to the
overwhelming passions of the heart and the
unconquerable realities of life until, at last,
he is forced to his knees and confesses that
there is a God. In this, as in Robert
Elsmere, although the finale be in the
opposite direction, the same eternal and
irrepressible theme—man's relation to the
something beyond himself—gives it all the
perspective and the color of its interest.

It is a fair sample of its class, and may stand as an illustration of all.

But it is in the realistic novel, that apostolate of the ugly, that subjectivism reaches its final and fullest expression. In this school, the school of Zola and Ibsen, there is a studied endeavor to ignore or minimize the supernatural in men's lives. It paints life down to the most disgusting minutiæ and the most trivial details, and shuns the ideal as a pest. It aims at social reform by laying open, with the deliberate hand of a surgeon, the festering sores in the social body, and traces without scruple or tremor the revolting effects of vicious living. But it does all this, we are told, in the solemn interest of truth, in order that the picture of vice in the everyday life of men, may arouse them to a realization of the dreadful disease which afflicts the social body. The terrible effects of drunkenness, of lust and the wrongs, which a stupid conventionalism has fixed and perpetuated, are the uninviting subjects which it portrays in the leaden colors of the commonplace. It holds up the mirror of its vice to the world with an excruciating exactness and in painful detail. It purposely abandons the ideal and displays corrupted human nature, bald, nude and filthy. Such is its profession, and as far as possible, its practice.

But notwithstanding this studied attempt on the part of the realistic school to ignore the ideal, and therefore, the supernatural in man's life, the background of its sombre picture is made up of the very elements it professedly seeks to reject. It is only dreadful, only disgusting because the measure of its degradation is the ideal conception of what man should be. It is the implied absence of the beautiful, the lack of that moral consonance in man's life that makes the pages of realism so dark and revolting. It is because the Christian world has arrived at the conception that men's bodies are God's temples to be kept pure and undefiled, that it shudders to see them made the abode of all foulness and wickedness. Strike out of men's minds the Christian conception of what human life should be, and the realistic picture of its wickedness becomes a grotesque fantasy. In a community without the

Christian ideal it would be meaningless; to Turks or Chinese it would be incomprehensible.

Thus it is with all art, whether it takes the form of literature or not. It is ever measured by the ideal, and the supreme ideal is ever the product of the supernatural. Even when men turn away from that ideal and seek to deny the supernatural, their negation or their denial finds its only reason in the positive truth it would destroy. The nearer men are to the supernatural the closer do they approach to the ideal, and in proportion to their realization of the ideal do they approximate the beautiful. And as art is the sensible expression of the beautiful, the highest art will be found when and where men live in closest communion with the supernatural and the ideal. Subjectivism is the abandonment of the supernatural, a turning away from that something which is without and beyond humanity, and in the realistic novel we see it in its completest manifestation. But even here it is forced to confess to the ideal, for it is the previous conception of the beautiful, of health and

goodness that has given men any notion of
their negations.   Men would never have
known what disease is if they had never
realized what health is.   There never would
have been any realism in literature if there
had never been any falling away from the
Catholic ideal.

We are living at the height of the subjective movement.   Its full flood is now
sweeping over the modern world.   Man,
conscious of his own blindness, is groping
about for light ; knowing his own weakness,
is crying out for help ; or else, bloated by
his pride, is blindly proclaiming his fancied
omnipotence.   Because he has cut himself
off from the supernatural and sought to
build the universe out of his own power,
there has come upon him this confusion of
tongues.   In the political and the social
world, theory clashes with theory, utopia
with utopia, and salvation is sought, not
in the supernatural, but in the natural—in
distracted humanity—vainly seeking to lift
itself into a millennial heaven by virtue of
its own forces.   Subjectivism was never
more widespread, more virulent or more

forgetful of the higher life of man. That grand relation of man, first to God and then to his fellow-men, has been stricken out of its category of knowledge. But withal, subjectivism has never been weaker, for it has arrived at the term of its journey. It has conducted man to the frontiers of its own nescience, and left him on the edge of the unfathomable abyss. It is not in human nature not to recoil from these dreadful depths, and the very ignorance of himself, which subjectivism has so baldly displayed to him, is the surest pledge of his return. Not death but life he wants, not darkness but light he seeks. The final dictum, *I know not*, will never satisfy the cravings of his intellect, and when the sense of his own impotence presses closely upon his heart and his mind, will he not turn and throw himself once more into the everlasting arms of Catholic truth?

SCIENCE.

THEOLOGY, THE LIGHT OF LITERATURE.

In the opening of the previous paper
I spoke of literature as the written expression
of man's various relations to God and to his
fellow-men.   It was also said that the grand
relation of man is not first to his brother-man,
but to something that is beyond humanity—
to God; and that on the solemn and profound
beliefs arising out of this relation, all the
higher art of the world has based itself.
Correlative with this is the profound truth
that as man conceives of his relations to God,
so will he conceive and estimate his relations
to his fellow-men, and that the various great
relations which arise out of his domestic,
social and civil life find their roots in that
prime relation of his religious existence.   As
that same Spanish writer,* whom we before
quoted, has said : "Theology is the light of

---

* Donoso Cortés.

history;" that is, the light of human existence ; for, history, here used in its widest
sense, embraces all that belongs to humanity.
As literature is the written expression of
man's relation, first to God, and then to his
fellow-men, we will find the basis of his
literature resting upon his theology, and the
character of that literature will be fashioned
according to the nature of his theology.
When we understand the theology of a
people, that is, their knowledge and their
conception of their relation to the Divine
Being, we are on the way to a proper appreciation of their literary art, and not until we
have arrived at an appreciative understanding
of this vital connection between religion and
art, has the philosophy of literature any
meaning for us.

Literature, I have said, is art. As the
word art is often abusively applied in our
day, it will be well to make its meaning clear
and precise.

Unless we achieve,—I say achieve, for,
we only attain what is worth gaining by
rightly directed effort and persistent toil,—
unless we achieve those heights of under-

standing from which we may take in the full prospect of human knowledge, at least in a general way, and from which that fundamental and original unity of all the departments of man's intellectual and ethical life becomes visible, we will neither comprehend the true nature of art nor philosophically appreciate the real character of literature. In a series of studies of the present character, and indeed in any estimate of literature as the written expression of man's relations to divine and human things, our conception of the nature and purpose of art becomes the necessary keynote of our understanding of literature.

But we can not comprehend the nature of art until we have learned to understand its foundations in man's divine science, the consummation of all his knowledge, the beginning and end of his intellectual life. The relation here is essential and vital. We must comprehend that relation before we can proceed further.

Plato said that Beauty is the splendor of Truth. This is a literary rather than a metaphysical definition. It has, however,

an admirable aptness for our purpose, though
it may not enjoy the exactness of metaphysical science. Art, we have said, is the
sensible expression of beauty. Art, then, is
the sensible expression of the splendor of
truth. Before expanding the implications of
our definition, which we will reserve for
another study, let us note the intimate
relation between art and truth, a connection
which has been so often neglected in our
day, that it is forgotten, and being forgotten,
as often denied. It is in this heresy that we
may discover the cause of the degeneracy
and of the failure of modern art, which in
the school of Realism, its final outcome, lays
down, as its prime dogma, the solemn
absurdity that art is the sensible expression
of the ugly. In the decadence, which realism
most completely illustrates, we see the
exemplification of the so often ignored truth,
that the intellectual attitude of men invaria-
bly finds its practical manifestation in their
words and their deeds. As men think,
so will they do. Their beliefs and their
theories soon become their practice, and
the good or bad of their theories will

make the good or bad of their deeds.
The unity of human nature is self-assertive,
and who denies this unity is the first to
attest it in his actions. Whosoever declares
that theory is one thing and practice quite
another, utters a theoretical proposition
which he is forever putting into practice.
While he affirms that practice should be
divorced from theory, he is actually wedding
practice with theory, for, what does he do
other than to assume the proposition that
there should be no correspondence between
man's intellectual attitude in the affairs of
life and the execution of these affairs;
and what is this but to make a theory,
which he is ever putting into practical
effect. Man can never escape from his
theory of living, even when he imagines
that he is deliberately eschewing it, so indissoluble is the bond of human thought
with human action. For man is essentially
rational, and must, perforce, shape his conduct by the intellectual prospect of life
which his reason manifests to him. To deny
the intimate and effective correspondence
between his thought and his deed, between

his theory, whatever it may be, and his practice, is an intolerable contradiction, to which his reason refuses submission, and which his reason, in the very act of denial, nullifies.

As therefore, between the intellectual and the practical world, there is an intimate union, the very denial of which in the intellectual order is its affirmation, we may aver, that between the science of man and the practice of man there is an indissoluble bond. I use the word science, not in its narrower and restricted sense as a body of mere physical facts and theories, which is the present unfortunate vogue of the term, but as the systematized summation of all human knowledge and beliefs in the natural and revealed orders. In man, word and deed are but the issue of thought and belief. What he denies in his intellect, he will deny in his deed, and what he affirms with his intellect, he will affirm in his deed. But if man's science be not true science, true thought and true belief, if it have no foundation in the constitution of things, in the world of thought as well as in the world

of fact, in the world above man as well as
below him, it is of no avail; and in so far as
it is untrue, it will issue in false words and
false deeds. That we may truly understand
his literature, we must understand his
science in the supreme sense of the word,
that is, we must understand the sum of his
knowledge of himself in all the relations of
his existence. The final sum of that knowledge is, widely speaking, his theology, his
conception of his primal and final relation
to the divine.

There have been and are, speaking
broadly and avoiding the futility of details,
four different stages of theological conviction and expression in man's history.

He regards nature as divine; peoples
all its various parts with gods; the lights
of heaven become deities; the deeps of the
abyss are alive with the mysteries of the
divinities; the whirlwind and the zephyr
are the wrathful or the gentle breathing of
the gods; mountain top and valley are the
fanes of superior beings, demanding pro-
pitiation and worship from man; the majesty of ocean acknowledges a special divine

ruler, on whose pleasure the awed voyager depends for his safety; the running stream and the raining heavens, the depths of the forests and the open spaces of the fields have their allotted divine guardians, whose care is jealous and whose vengeance is swift; earth and air, fire and water teem with deified presences, and man bows before them all, the humble suitor for their favor, or the sacrilegious victim of their wrath. In presence of the forces of nature man feels himself weak : Nature cherishes him at one moment with her fecundity, and smites him the next in the whirlwind and the lightning. He fixes his adoration upon her powers, so much mightier than himself. He attributes a personality and a will to exterior objects, whose acts are not his own, and adores them. This is Paganism. Here nature is God.

Emancipated in time from the thralldom of the worship of nature, man comes to learn that he is nature's sovereign. The lightnings before which he once fell prostrate in fear as before a God, when they smote the quaking earth with noises that stunned and

confounded, he has learned by the cunning
of his intellect to wield in his own hand.
Jupiter Tonans is thrust from his throne,
and man, in his own puny fingers, grasps
the dead god's thunder-bolts. The majestic
wrath of the turbulent seas he has subdued
to the power of his iron leviathans. The
tornado and the whirlwind, at whose mercy
his audacious cockle-shell once tossed above
the roaring abysses that menaced him from
below, he now sails through in scornful
confidence by the might of the power of a
drop of water, which he has summoned from
the fountains of nature to do the bidding of
his will. Space and time he has epitomized
into a miraculous brevity. He has made the
journey of a year the jaunt of a week; he
talks across oceans and converses over the
breadth of continents; he has harnessed
subdued nature to his triumphant chariot,
and like a conqueror, all of whose enchained
rivals follow in the tracks of his triumph in
testimony of his victory, he places the crown
of sovereignty upon his own brow as a right
arising out of his own omnipotence. By the
power of his reason has he wrought this

world of wonders. Reason is king and lord
and master, nor in the heavens above nor in
the earth beneath is there anything like unto
him, save what he has made to his own likeness and fashioned to his own image, his
creatures and his slaves. And man falls
down and adores himself. This is the
theology we call Rationalism.

But after a little, man learns that his
sovereignty over nature is not complete. It
is a dependent rule. It is true that he can
subdue nature to his service, but only by
scrupulously and even fearfully complying
with the tyranny of forces, which are at the
same time blind and terrible. He pays for
his command over nature by submitting to
the exactions of an inexorable law ; swift
and fearful the retribution when he violates
that law. The tremendous power of the drop
of water expanded into vapor, which he
presses into his busy service, in a moment of
negligence or weakness may become the
instant instrument of his destruction. No,
he is not sovereign after all. When he
comes to consider closely, a mere nominal
master, who is in reality the slave of his

subjects, a conqueror, the victim of the conquered. While nature is serving him she
devours him, and in time completely destroys him. His kingdom is after all only
a realm of shades, his scepter the semblance
of rule ; his crown the bauble of a moment,
and his power the shadow of a substance.
So he lies the shattered column of what
was once a king—widowed of the brief
authority that erst shone in regal splendor
from his royal front.

    But human nature does not long suffer
defeat with meekness. Man longs for the
bright pre-eminence where his imagination
enthroned him as a god. If he be not
nature's sovereign, he is, at least, nature's
equal. Nature, whose secrets he has in part
wrested from her jealous bosom, can not be
more wonderful than human reason which
reads her story and interprets the lessons of
her power. Are not, after all, the mighty
forces that agitate and mould her frame, the
same forces that fashion and animate his? Is
it not the same universal force that mutters
in the thunder and speaks consciously in
his reason ? Not different from nature, but

one in substance with her ; not the fearful
slave of nature's despotism, but the sublimest
expression of nature's soul welling up into
consciousness and will in human reason,
the completest and profoundest elaboration of
her divine spirit : consubstantial and equal
man and nature—both are God in one.
Nature, as other than man and sovereign
over him, is not God, and man, as other
than nature and sovereign over her, is not
God, but man and nature, sovereign together,
constitute divinity. Paganism and Rationalism coalesce ; human pride is saved, and we
have the theology called Pantheism.

Outside of Christianity, which is the
fourth definite expression of human science,
Paganism, Rationalism and Pantheism fill
the measure of man's knowledge. In one or
the other of these ways has he ever answered
the problem of the universe, which is the
problem of human destiny, the one problem
of vital and eternal concern to him, the one
problem to which all his science is bent and
in which it concludes, the one problem upon
whose solution the conduct of his life depends
and upon which his destiny hangs. Only in

the light of his answer to this problem can his history be read, can his art be understood, or his literature be estimated. Some definite answer he has always given, according to which his word and his deed have been shaped. There is no race, no people that has not given an answer. I say no race, no people, because never yet has the spirit of skepticism possessed an entire people or nation, though there may be periods in their history when that spirit is temporarily in the ascendant, or at least of such influence as to chill and benumb the soul of belief into sluggishness and apathy. But when skepticism has power enough to paralyze the active life of a people's divine science, a period of decadence then sets in, blasting its fruit and flower as the cold breath of winter strips the landscape of the bloom of summer, leaving the fields bare and the forests gaunt. Where there is no science—I use the word science in its full and legitimate sense—there will be no art, no literature. Where skepticism has spread the leprosy of its doubt, corroding faith and destroying conviction, art decays and literature declines. At such a time you will find many copies of the great masters, but of great masters, few or none. Literature will degenerate into a mass of conventional criticism given to analyzing, comparing and cataloguing the genius which is past, but filled with the paralyzing spirit of its own doubt, incapable of reviving the greatness that out of faith once flamed into glory ; or when it seeks to produce, it will either conventionally imitate the dead past or descend to the level of the commonplace and the ugly, mistaking an accurate and detailed copy of human failings for art-work. Doubt never creates ; skepticism never acts ; agnosticism always destroys. The powers of negation are ever impotent ; doubt vacillates between truth and falsehood ; skepticism denies truth; agnosticism ignores it.

It is a solemn and inviolable truth that men must have faith and conviction before they can utter the positive word, the word instinct with creative power, or do the positive deed, the deed potent with great events. Human science must grasp the truth in some degree or manner before the human word or the human deed can express it, and just in proportion to its apprehension of truth will be its power to express it. Sterile the science, or rather the negation of science founded on doubt or denial of the ultimate validity of truth. Faith in ultimate truth, conviction of its objective existence, the sense of its power, the inspiration of its life, quickening and creating, must dwell within the soul of art before its splendor can manifest itself living in the word or deed. This conviction of the illuminating presence of truth has no vitality if it dwell merely in the abstract regions of speculation. To be fecund, it must permeate the soul, penetrate all its faculties, seize it, possess it, enkindle it, until it glow and flame into that visible splendor which men call art.

Science, the knowledge of divine things, encompassing all other things, is the root of art, the foundation of its achievements, the vivifying center of the glory radiating through the arches of heaven and illuminating the horizon of man's pilgrimage through the sounding valleys of sense.

Paganism, after its own kind, possessed

such a science. It was imperfect, broken,
dimmed, encompassed with shadows, encir-
cled with gloom, but it was positive and
sincere. It was a conviction and a faith.
It recognized the divine, even though confusedly and brokenly. It saw God in nature ;
it identified God with nature. It divided and
multiplied the divine everywhere. Heaven
and earth, ocean and air, tree and shrub,
field and hill, valley and mountain, stream
and sea were the abodes of the gods. Nature
was instinct with indwelling divinities in all
her parts as the outward embodiment of their
presence. And in this, there was the shadow
of a great truth ; it was the broken and
confused tradition—persistently lingering in
the blunted memory of the race—of that
distant time when man, in his primeval
innocence, walked and conversed in the
Garden of Eden with his Maker, and God
spoke familiarly with His creature ; for in
a particular manner did God manifest Himself on earth to Adam before the dissonance
of sin had rent asunder that golden chain of
harmony, in whose unbroken diapason earth
then swung concordantly pendent to heaven.

The echoes of that celestial music still lingered in the soul of paganism. It sang of nymph and faun and dryad and satyr, and in the darkness of its understanding, it confounded creation with its Creator; but it had, in this much, a science of divine things which included all other things, and it created an art and produced a literature—an art and a literature prodigal in their wealth of form and variety of expression. This science in divine things was the root of its art; its art, the efflorescence of its divine science.

Rationalism, in its way and in its degree, possesses a divine science. Unlike paganism, it has never grown, for of its own nature it cannot so grow, to an unmixed development amongst any race or people. It has its epochs and periods of sway, but not unresisted and undisputed. It made its appearance on the stage of the world long after Christianity had fixed and established the basis of modern society, and we can generally recognize it and measure its effects only as a power of limitation in contrast with the positive and sublime science of Christianity.

Still, as it is not utter denial and rises to the positive assertion of an incomplete truth, which paganism completely misses, in affirming the sovereignty of man over nature, and as it establishes a faith in the divinity of human reason, to which it refers all things and under which it includes all things, it possesses the advantage of a stable conviction, and, therefore, a power of articulate expression. With it, art and literature are possible, but hampered and constricted by the narrow limits of an incomplete affirmation beginning and ending in a self-assertive egoism. Its seed was sown in the sixteenth century, the century of revolt from the unity of science. In its incompleteness, it divided unity and narrowed art, and though it has not lacked a voluminous literature, its word has been one of protestation rather than of affirmation. As it swept onward through the seventeenth and eighteenth centuries, its current narrowed and shallowed until it issued in that terrible parody of itself, the image of its abasement, the expression of its final impotence, when human reason fell down

flat and worshipped itself in the person of
a harlot. The cold stones of Notre Dame
must have felt their insensate cores burn
with very shame in presence of that
profound infamy! Yet that memorable
degradation was an act of worship and a
confession, a confession before the tabernacle
of the Most High, for human nature needs
must come to the desecrated sanctuary of the
Holy of Holies to confess the human necessity of worship and its own nothingness! As
if Providence were constraining it to render
testimony against itself in the Judgment
Hall of the Supreme Reason. It was the
confession that man must adore something,
and if he will not adore the highest, he must
needs fall prostrate before the lowest. Paganism left him prostrate before the hoof of
Apis; Rationalism placed him prostrate
before the basest of his passions. Yet, even
here, man did not reach the deepest deep
nor sound the bottom of the farthest abyss,
for though he worshipped falsely and abjectly,
still he worshipped and, in an imperfect and
vicious manner, rendered divine homage.
It is only in the stagnation of skepticism, in

the nether void of Agnosticism, where he
neither adores nor has the wish to adore,
that his faculties become completely paralyzed
and the fountains of his life frozen up under
the fatal chill of isolation ! Skepticism not
only denies God, but it denies nature and it
denies reason. It sounds the knell of science.
It does not possess even the image of death ;
it is the very abyss of the void, without
shape, without form, the abode of silence,
the domain of emptiness, the region of
nothingness. I am far from saying that
skepticism ever reaches this utterly vacant
expression of its vanity. That were to make
possible the impossible, for nothingness can
never manifest itself save in one way only—
by destruction. It has no being, therefore
no truth, no science, no art, no literature ;
it expresses itself only in destruction and by
virtue of that which it would destroy. In
art, it denies beauty and exalts the ugly to
her high place. In literature, it begets—if a
negative can be said to beget—Realism, and
this much it does, not that it seeks to affirm
anything, but by way of so many steps in
the descent to the abyss.

But man was not made for annihilation.
Being was made for Being. Human reason,
hurled into the abyss of its own impotence
and abased in the weakness of its pride to
the worship of the senses, whence in sheer
despair it plunges into the chaos of skepticism, revolts and turns from the confusions
of nescience. To salve the wound of its
pride and fill the void, that alone it could
not fill, it turns again to nature, not as a
suppliant and fearful slave, but as one in
substance and essence with nature's self.
From its self-defeat Reason takes refuge in
Pantheism. Here is a fuller affirmation than
Rationalism utters—a completer declaration
than Paganism voices. It possesses a divine
science under which it includes all other
things. Its conviction is positive ; it has a
power of expression. It can manifest itself in
art and in literature. In proportion to its
power to utter itself—a capacity in ratio
with the universality of its scheme—must we
measure the extent of its influence and the
reach of its domination. It is the profoundest
and the subtlest, and therefore the most dan-
gerous of all the errors of rebellious human

nature. It avoids the dangers of the abyss
of nescience into which Rationalism ulti-
mately leads ; it transcends the fatal slavery
to the blind forces of nature which Paganism imposes upon man. It talks of God
and man and nature, of soul and of spirit
and of freedom with perfervid eloquence; it
transfigures everything into divine manifestations of deity ; it sees in history the evolu-
tion of a Providence ; it recognizes the
sacredness of Religion everywhere and at all
times ; man and his institutions are in its
eyes phases in the development of divine life
in the world ; all things are true; falsity is
but the temporary limitation of the manifestations of the divine truth in things,
gradually unfolding itself like the leaves of
the rose from the immature bud ; good is
essentially in all things ; all things are
essentially good ; evil, like truth, is but the
limitation of present environment seeking
expression in time and in space—eternal
forms of universal and infinite existence. It
has all the pride of Rationalism, all the
abjectness of Paganism. With the former,
it declares the supremacy of reason ; with

the latter, the sovereignty of nature, and reconciles their antagonism by making them identical in an Hegelian formula. It is all things to all men; accounts for all things to all men in every man's way and according to each man's view; for all errors are its errors; all truth it claims to be its truth, so capacious is its embrace, so wide its capacity. In short, it makes all things God save God Himself.

But in its denial of God as Sovereign, Lord and Master of man and nature, distinct from them as Creator is distinct from creature by an infinite abyss, it makes the supreme denial, the denial that is death. It has not arrived at the fullness of truth, as it imagines, in transcending the limitations of reason on the one hand and the shortcomings of nature on the other, by syncopating them into one. The infinite is never reached by the coalescence of two finites. This is merely a process of widening the limits of the finite—an indefinite extension of that which is always finite. For the finite is not finite because it has limits, but has limits because it is finite; and however far you may project it into the imaginary regions of the indefinite, it ever carries with it the essential nature of the finite, and therefore the limitations which necessarily arise from its finite constitution. The impotence of reason on the one hand, and the impotence of nature on the other hand to supply the fullness of truth, do not become omnipotence by combination. By multiplying human nature indefinitely you do not get the angelic nature, nor by multiplying the angelic nature indefinitely do you get the divine. The sum of their impotences simply widens the sphere of their incapacities to manifest the absolute. It is in this confusion of quantity with essence and of the indefinite with the infinite that Pantheism confounds the imagination and disorders the mind. In the world of literature, whose immediate organ of expression is the imagination, this radical confusion spreads with subtle and characteristic influence, especially when stimulated by that wide sympathy for nature and humanity which Pantheism so readily and fluently sublimates into a universal sentimentalism. It takes the trained metaphysical eye to detect the error and unravel the confusion, and trained metaphysicians are as rare in the literary world to-day as in ancient days were chaste matrons in the salacious cities by the Dead Sea.

And modern literature is striking its roots deep down into Pantheistic science. It is into the Pantheistic stream that all the currents of modern thought are for the most part flowing. Rationalism and Skepticism, though at times noisy and raucous, are only shore eddies in the sweep of the waters. The inadequacy of Rationalism to solve the problem of human existence and to supplement man's religious aspirations has become manifest; the absolute sterility of nescience in human life in every respect is now made evident, and the world, wearied by the vanity of the one, and revolted against the inanity of the other, is turning to the wide promise and the alluring prospects of Pantheism. The closing decade of the nineteenth century is witness to this turn in the tide; it is voicing the failure of Rationalism and Skepticism, and already begins to chant the pæan of the new theology, the tramp of whose marching hosts is even now making the earth vibrate. As the eighteenth century saw the career of Rationalism, as the nineteenth witnessed the disastrous sweep of skeptical agnosticism, so will the twentieth usher in the seismic wave of Pantheism, and if we may measure the fluctuations of modern thought in the future by the varying phenomena of its rise and fall in the past, the same century will see that flood recede into the abysses of human pride.

There now remains another positive expression of divine science, which I have purposely reserved for the concluding consideration of our present discourse. I have reserved it for the last, because all that the others lack, it possesses in prolific fullness and in a supereminent manner; moreover, because unlike them, it is not of human making, but of divine constitution. Unlike them, it does not issue from the abyss of human pride and the emptiness of human thought, but descends from the heights of Divine Love and the omniscience of the Divine Intellect; it alone explains the origin

of all things, and points their completed
term ; it alone accounts for man's beginning
and end ; illuminates the path of his earthly
peregrination, gives reason for his sufferings,
understands his sighs and his tears, allevi-
ates his burdens, directs his stumbling foot-
steps with unerring knowledge, confirms his
weakness and lifts him when he falls.*   It
alone reads the painful riddle of the earth in
the light of its dogmas of sin and redemption, and solves the dark enigma of the
world's disorders in the harmonies of its
doctrines of the expiatory virtue of penalty
and the redeeming power of grace.   And all
this it does in the light of its divine science,
which transcends human knowledge in an
absolute manner and differs from it in a
transcendent manner.   For human knowledge, in consequence of the constitutional
limitations of the human intellect, illuminating only within the narrow expanse of its
contracted compass, ever leads us up to the
mysterious confines of its brief power and
leaves us apalled in presence of an impene-

* Donoso Cortés: Essays on Socialism, Catholicism and Lib-
eralism; Book I., Chap. 2 "Of Society Under the Empire of
Catholic Theology."

trable exterior darkness, in whose profound encircling night the flickering torch of human reason burns like a minute spark in an illimitable abyss.

Unlike human science going from imperfect knowledge to profound mystery, Catholic science goes from profound mystery to perfect knowledge, and, strange to say, reversing the order of human things where light is ever swallowed in darkness, the reason of its profound mystery lies in its transcendent light; for so great is the ineffable virtue of the Catholic mysteries that, though in themselves opaque, all things else are made transcendently clear by their illumination; and, stranger still to say, were they not opaque to human reason, they would not possess that power of transcendent illumination; for, if in their essence they were visible to human reason and measurable by it, they would be subject to its limitations and coincident with all its impotence. If, then, they were comprehensible by the human intellect, they would cease to be mysteries, and ceasing to be mysteries, they would no longer throw their penetrating and clarifying light upon

that interior and exterior darkness which so
profoundly penetrates and encompasses the
human mind ; but merely conducting man
to the frontiers of his ignorance, leave him
there overwhelmed and crushed by the sense
of his own weakness. For it is of the essential
nature of a mystery to be above reason and
transcending reason illuminate it, though
itself be not illuminated.

Such is Catholic science, founded upon
luminous mysteries, whose light penetrates
all things but is in itself impenetrable. It
reconciles nature and man, not by confounding one with the other, but by subordinating
the one to the other in the hierarchy of
creatures by virtue of the supreme sovereignty of their common Creator. In this
way does it save human reason from the
abasement of Rationalism, which ever falls
into the pit of pride, where it is continually
devoured by Skepticism ; and from the
fatalism of Pantheism, which, while seeking
to save reason from the distress of Rationalism and the tyranny of nature by combining
their despotisms, plunges man into the
deeper abyss of necessity; for human freedom

is only saved from the iron thralldom of
nature on the one hand, and from its own fatal
limitations on the other, by virtue of a free
power greater than either and sovereign over
both, in which the necessities of the one and
the limitations of the other find a common
term, resolving the one and exalting the
other. The reason for this lies first, in the
fact that, it is only in God that reason
escapes the necessities of nature ; for, in God
—the end—nature the instrument ceases to
be of service, having fulfilled its complete
purpose as the rational creature's means to
the accomplished end ; and second, in the
fact that it is only in God—the Supreme
Reason—that finite reason finds its own
limitations transcended, and is exalted by an
intimate union which receives and yet preserves it unconfounded.

In Rationalism, reason claiming absolute
sovereignty contemned and despised nature,
and nature, resenting as it were, the heel of
an unauthorized usurper, turned and smote
him groveling to the earth. In Pantheism,
reason, finding its claim to sovereignty
disputed and opposed, seeks to make that

claim good by yielding it, and, descending from its throne to the lower levels of nature, sacrifices its dignity by identifying it with an inferior. In Christianity, reason, claiming title of vice-regent only by virtue of a power greater and beyond its own, subordinates and uses nature as a pathway to a nobler freedom, preserving its dignity in humility and perfecting its power in infirmity.

In this way, Catholic science establishes the hierarchy of knowledge and preserves the unity of science, comprehends the order of the universe, reconciles the disorder wrought by the ravages of sin, lifts man from the abyss of impotence, and, out of his own unworthiness, draws him to the heights of omnipotence, without sacrificing his liberty or dissolving his identity. But all this, only Catholic science can accomplish. From its perennial fountains has gushed the copious stream of the sublimest art and the greatest literature of mankind, wonderful in the unity and sublimity of their manifestation, and at the same time as varied in their expression as the different

peoples amidst whom they have burgeoned.
Like Paganism, it sees the divine in nature,
not confused and confounded, but as the
external manifestation of its Maker's beauty
and power and wisdom and goodness ; and,
unlike Paganism intoxicated with the joy of
the glory of visible things, it lifts man beyond
the veils of sense in hope and aspiration to
the invisible goods, of which these are but
the promise.   Like Rationalism, it exalts
reason above the blind powers of nature and
proclaims the superior dignity of man over
all creatures about him, but, unlike Rationalism building in pride on its own nothingness, it founds that dignity not in an absolute
self-sovereignty over nature, but in a vice-
regency holding all its title of power from the
sovereign will of a common Creator.   Like
Pantheism, it sees the unity of man and
nature, but unlike Pantheism mistaking
identity for unity, it establishes that unity
in a hierarchy of creatureship bound together
under the one sovereignty of a Supreme
Master, who has subordinated the one to the
other in order to a common term.   Unlike
Paganism, Rationalism and Pantheism, only

it and it alone comprehends the radical diffi-
culty in human nature, points out its source
in sin, supplies its failure by grace, and
encompasses its disorder by a higher order,
accomplishing that miracle of wisdom and of
power, of drawing good out of evil without
interfering with the disorder in sin and without destroying human liberty.

Rooted deep down in the fecund soil of
this wonderful Catholic science, the art and
literature of Christendom have drawn their
vigorous sustenance and their exalted power.
Even the rebellions against it have found
their sole virtue in having once drawn their
sap from that prolific stem. The civilization of
the day has been elaborated by the power and
spirit of that same divine science ; the warp
and woof of our social texture is spun from
its looms ; our domestic existence is fashioned
and formed upon its model. As out of it
grows our life, so out of it grows our literature—the written expression of our life—and
even when assaulting it under the various
standards of rebellion, bears witness to its
constraining virtue and lofty ideal; for all
the   modern   rebellions   against   Catholic

science either borrow the substance of their power and their expression, if positive at all, from some fragment of Catholic truth, or gain a hearing and a negative vantage only by virtue of vehemently protesting against some positive element in its universal constitution.

To sum up, we may say that in religion, wherein is the complete expression of man's relation to God, is to be found the beginning and end of human wisdom. As man conceives that prime and final relation, so will he draw from it as from the fountain head, his notions of his relations to his fellow-men, of the rights and duties of his life, the rule and measure of his conduct. Resting upon that eternal foundation are the bases of his art-work and his literature. As he thinks, he lives, and as he lives, he speaks; as his science, so his life, and as his life, his literature—the spoken word of his life. His theology is the divine science of his life—the alpha and omega of the sum of his knowledge, and in this way we find his theology the light of his literature.

ART.

The Sensible Expression of Unity by Variety.

We have seen how profoundly art is rooted in man's divine science, how universally true it is that theology is the light of literature. Now that we have come to understand how intimate and essential is the relation between science and art, and therefore between science and literature, discerning in that relation the secret springs of man's word about himself and the universe, we naturally betake ourselves to a further inquiry into the meaning of the term art, which we have used with one invariable signification. That meaning we briefly defined in our last discourse, but had no opportunity to amplify.

It is to the explication of the meaning of art, and in an especial sense of literature as art, that I now wish to address myself. It was said in our last discourse, that art was

the sensible expression of the beautiful, and
we accepted the Platonic definition or description of beauty as the splendor of truth. This
we called a literary rather than a strictly
metaphysical definition, yet with all the
virtues of our purpose. We occupied ourselves with showing how the art of literature
depended upon man's conception of truth
expressed in his divine science or in his theology. His theology, we saw, is the expression
of the sum of his knowledge of the truth.
But it is not his artistic expression of that
truth. Truth finds its expression amongst
men not only in the abstract formulæ of the
intellect—in the pure white light of speculation in which the eye of the simple intellect
contemplates it—but descends from those
arid heights into the concrete atmosphere of
the imagination which, like a prism, breaks
the pure ray into many colors over the varied
vistas of sensible existence. By imagination
I do not mean mere fancy, but that highest
of man's organic faculties, by which he
concretely epitomizes into variedly multiplied
and combined images, called phantasms by
the metaphysicians, the entire external world

coming within his sensible perception. So
closely and intimately is this faculty asso-
ciated with the operations of the intellect,
that save to the acute dialectician there is
danger of confounding the two, yet between
them, as psychology amply demonstrates,
there is the wide abyss of that tremendous
difference which distinguishes and separates
the spiritual from the material order, man
from the brute.

We can always, however, save ourselves
from confusion, even if we be not metaphysicians, by carrying in our minds this broad
and simple distinction : the phantasm of the
imagination is the concrete and particular
picture of the sensible object ; the intellectual
image is the abstract universal concept of the
object stripped of all its sensible qualities.
The imagination of man, though generically
the same as in the brute, enjoys this vast
difference : its vital principle is spiritual ;
the same soul which exercises the faculty of
thought in the intellect, is ths same soul
which animates the body and radically
exercises its organic powers. Moreover, the
human imagination, thus again differing

from the brute's, is ordained to the intellectual life as the proximate* medium of the
intellect's communication with the external
world. In the brute, the sole function of
the imagination is to combine its various
sensations into the single concrete picture by
which its physical life may be sensibly
guided and conserved. But in man, the
imagination is immensely ennobled both by
the superior principle which animates it and
by its intimate ordination to the intellectual
world. Here the concrete image is illuminated by an intellectual light, under whose
spiritualizing ray its grosser elements are
sublimated, falling away as it were from the
subtle spirit of the essence; and the essence
thus denuded of its sensible properties, is
prepared to be received into the abstract
regions of the speculative order, where, as
concept of the intellect, it becomes the
universal. In its turn, the imagination,
inundated as it were by the fecund ray of
the intellectual light, permeated and vivified
by it, receives the psychic illumination of
the superior power into the endless variety of

---

* Proximate to the Intellect.

its imagery, embodying it in figure and form, kindling it into color and flame. Here in the human imagination, correlated with the intellect, is the region of art, the region of the sensible expression of the beautiful, of the visible splendor of truth.

We must be careful to note that the imagination, apart from its relation to the intellect, is not the faculty of art expression. Without this subordination and relation to the higher life of the intellect, the imagination, deprived of the co-ordinating and unitive power of the superior faculty, degenerates into mere fancy—the region of the fantastical and the disorderly, in whose arbitrary and unrelated combinations, lurid with the glow of passion and distraught by mere caprice, beauty is eclipsed and truth darkened. It is only by virtue of the higher light that the imagination, so illuminated, dominated, regulated, controlled, becomes the art faculty with power to give sensible expression to the beautiful. It is, therefore, in and through the imagery of the imagination, translucent with the serene ray of intellectual light, that the splendor of truth

glows in all the rich variety of the form and
color of the sensible world. And in this we
see how essential and how vital is the
dependence of art upon science, for if that
science be false and incomplete, the imagination will receive a false and obscured illumination, making shadow and confusion in the
vast galleries of its imagery.

But the intellect and the imagination of
man draw, the one its ideas, and the other
its images from the external world about
him. Truth is not of man's own making,
nor beauty of his own imagining. Both
come to him from without; both he apprehends through their manifestations in the
world external to him. His faculties are
adjusted to their reception and to their
expression in his deed and in his word, but
their creation is not his. The visible universe
sensibly reveals itself to him in time and
in space. Uncreate beauty manifests itself
through and in the visible universe. Condescending to the weakness of human faculties, it softens its glories to our finite
capacities in the world of sense. For time
and space are the barriers of the sensible

world, marking off the boundaries of the eternal and the infinite; it is through these veils that the invisible order manifests itself to us after the manner of our present existence.* Uncreate beauty, which is absolute and infinite, condescending to our state, and sacrificing its immensities and its intimate glories, enters into the boundaries of time and space, that under their softening shadows our finite faculties may find power to gaze upon its reflected beauty without being consumed by its splendors.

But time and space are subject to law. We may say that their law is the law of the manifestation of beauty in the sensible world. In making itself visible to man, uncreate beauty accepts in a manner the limitations of time and space; but this it does not only by way of condescension to the weakness of human capacities, but as the necessary condition of its visibility in the sensible order; for beauty is made visible to human eyes

---

* "Le temps et l'espace gardent les barrières de ce monde et saisissent tout ce qui veut entrer. Rien ne leur échappe. Aussi sans violer son unité, l'Art doucira-t-il ses splendeurs immenses et complaisantes pour les accomoder à notre spécialité humaine." —Ernest Hello, "L'Homme," Livre III., "L'Art."

only in time and in space and only by
conformity with their laws. Therefore do
we find the art world essentially and necessarily subject to law and order. The sensible
expression of beauty must be in accord either
with the law of time or the law of space.
Now time, in art, is the sensible expression
of succession; the law of the science of
numbers is its government. Beauty, under
the law of time, manifests itself in con-
cordant measure or rhythm, and divides its
expression into poetry and music.

Space, in art, is the sensible expression
of co-existence. The law of the science of
extension is its government. Beauty, under
the law of space, manifests itself in the
measures of proportion made visible by light,
and divides its expression into architecture,
sculpture and painting. In this way does
the sensible world come into the service of
the idea, administering to its manifestation
in the human word and in light. At the
same time, that administration is according
to the law of sensible being and dependent
upon that law, for save in due accord with
that law, the idea can never be made visible

in the regions of matter. But whilst the
idea is thus made manifest according to the
law of the visible world of space and time,
and only by observing the obligations of
that law, the idea at the same time imposes
its own higher law upon that sensible expression of its splendor in the external world.
That higher law is unity.

Art, we have said, is the sensible
expression of beauty, and beauty we have
called the splendor of truth. But truth is
one, absolute; in the amplitude of its infin-
ity, it is all things without the differences
of many things. It is one absolute and
indivisible, one infinite and eternal, possess-
ing in absolute and in indivisible unity an
infinite perfection, wherein, in a supereminent way, it contains the perfections of all
beings, without their limitations and their
differences. Inexhaustible, therefore, on the
one hand, is the power of the manifestation
of infinite unity in the sensible universe and
limitless the variety of its expression; on
the other hand, impossible that there should
be any expression of perfection in the universe of time and space, that does not in

some species of external variety, show forth
that indivisible perfection of the absolute and
the infinite. Whatever be that expression in
the external universe, the sole law of its perfection lies in the power of its entity, in the
degree and kind of its variety, to give sensible expression to the splendor of absolute
truth. As beauty is the splendor of truth,
as truth is absolute unity, supereminently
containing all the perfections of being, the
law of beauty in the visible order consists in
the manifestation of the unity of truth in
sensible variety. Space and time supply the
visible forms of variety as vehicles for the
splendor of the idea, by the virtue of whose
supreme unity this inexhaustible variety is
co-ordinated and vivified into one organic
whole. In this do we discover the supreme
law of art, unity in variety and variety in
unity.

This is the supreme law of art, because
it is the supreme law of truth, and it is the
supreme law of truth, because it is the
supreme law of life. The universe is its
visible expression, the sensible manifestation
in the external order of supreme unity per-

petually begetting variety, the radiated splendor of absolute unity forever generating absolute variety in its own eternal bosom. In the unity of the Divine Substance is a perpetual trinity of Divine Persons. In this Divine Variety, springing perennially from this Divine Unity, is the intrinsic manifestation of the Divine Glory, the absolute Being forever dilating into perfect Power, Wisdom and Love. The One forever One, and yet Three forever out of One as their eternal origin ; the Three forever Three and yet forever in One ; infinite distinction out of infinite unity ; infinite unity forever expressing itself in infinite variety.

This is the ineffable mystery of supreme truth and supreme life. It is the hidden law of all truth and of all life, not indeed manifest to us in its own essence, but manifesting all things to us. It has been made known to us not that we may see into it, but that we may see by it. It is the law of the government of the Divine Nature, and it is by participation the law of the government of the universe visible and invisible. "This occult law," says Donoso Cortés, "which presides at the generation of unity and variety must be the highest, most universal, most excellent and mysterious of all, as God has subjected to it all things, human and divine, created and uncreated, visible and invisible. Being one in its essence, it is infinite in its manifestations ; everything that exists appears to exist only to manifest it, and each one of the things that exists manifests it in a different way. It is one way in God, another in God made man, another in His Church, another in the family, another in the universe; but it is in all and in each and every part. Here it is an invisible and incomprehensible mystery, and there, without ceasing to be a mystery, it is a visible phenomenon and palpable fact.''

As this variety in unity is the supreme law of truth and life, so is it for that reason, the supreme law of art, for art, as we have seen, is but the sensible expression of the splendor of truth, and, therefore, the law of truth must be its law. The law that governs in the domain of truth must be the law that presides over the manifestation of its splendor in the region of art. The unity between truth and art is essential, the law of their

unity one, and their very variety a manifestation of their unity, for in one way is the
same law manifested in the intellect which is
the region of truth, and in another way in
the imagination which is the region of art.
In the intellectual world, it shows forth in
the variety of the intellectual operations of
the one power apprehending the one truth
conceived in a multitude of ideas, the word of
the mind variously receiving and expressing
the unity of truth as it is inexhaustibly and
manifoldly bodied forth in the multiplicity of
created being; in the world of the imagination, where lies the domain of art, it bursts
into the iridescent splendors of that same
truth, variously embodied in the sensible
forms of time and space across the ever-
shifting vistas of mutable and contingent
existence.

It is the law of life, manifesting itself
in a living growth. In the world of art, it
is the living principle of all true accomplish-
ment, for art must be living to be art at
all. In a particular and intimate sense
is art said to be creative. It is a living
power that takes to itself the elements of its

expression, assimilates them to its own being
and gives them forth instinct with its own
life. It begets its own living image in endless variety. To substitute the rule or the
formula for this law of life is to construct a
mechanism, not to develop an organism.
Art has no rule or formula, or rather the
government of expression in art is the
intimate law of its own essence and precedes
the rule or formula, which follows from it,
and without its vital principle becomes but
the empty husk of its departed spirit. It is
at the luminous center of this living law that
genius dwells with power to create. Genius
knows the law and abides in it, but neither
knows nor tolerates formulæ. Talent seizes
upon the rule, the deserted chrysalis of the
soul of genius fled, mechanizes it, applies the
measure and constructs an artifice in wax, in
imitation of the beauty of the living rose
blown to fragrance and sweetness and
resplendent color by the creative power of
genius.

It is by virtue of this same supreme law
governing the expression of unity by variety,
that we find our delight in the visible mani-

festation of beauty in the world of art. The intellect comprehends the unity of things, the imagination apprehends their variety. These interfused powers, the scope of whose action lies in the world of art, æsthetically combine the unity in variety and expand the variety in unity of the visible universe, and in this largess of beauty, thus made manifest to it, the soul, filled with the delight of the divine harmony, is lifted upon the wings of contemplation to the fleeting vision of that supreme glory, whose vestment is time and space concealing while revealing and revealing while concealing it from mortal eyes.

Wherever there be unity in variety and variety in unity, the soul will delight in it. This is the secret of the pleasure of harmony and melody; harmony being the consentaneous union of various musical sounds, and melody their successive concordance upon a common key-note. This is the secret of the pleasure of rhythm in verse, for rhythm is not a mere mechanical contrivance of syllables arbitrarily placed, but the natural expression of lofty sentiment and noble

thought, seeking manifestation in the music
of words under the impulse of this secret
law of beauty, dilating unity into variety and
combining variety into unity. In the regu-
lar cadence of the line, modulated long or
short as it may be, we have unity; in the
differing quantity of each measure, variety.
The poet naturally expresses himself in
rhythm; indeed, rhythm is the exigency of
his utterance. The heat of his imagination,
which glows with the splendor of beauty,
fuses the structure of language to the measure of the music beating in his soul. Prose
to him is an inadequate and imperfect
expression; it has no measured succession
of harmonious variety where the law of
beauty may freely manifest itself according to
the needs of its being. His utterance must be
song; he transcends the irregularity of prose.
Nothing can be further from the truth than
the vulgar notion that the poet dwells outside of the region of law and order. He,
above all others, must submit himself to the
exactions of the rigorous laws governing the
sensible manifestations of beauty, as he has
no utterance at all save in that rhythmical

mode which the law of time imposes upon
him, and whose yoke alone beauty in the
expression of the word submits to bear.
Not lawless but lawful is poetry. Its law is
a hidden and a higher law, binding with an
obligation that suffers no deflection from the
serene and inflexible line of its orbit around
the center of truth. That line, indeed, is
not visible to the common eye, which is
prone to ignore and deny the unseen, and
when it perceives effects transcending the
region of the commonplace, within whose
narrow horizon it forever moves, attributes the luminous phenomena to irregular-
ities and deviations from the small regula-
tions of its own plebeian nature. Even
the writer of prose cannot altogether escape
the law of unity in variety and variety in
unity, though, indeed, he is bound by it
in a much lesser degree than the poet.
Though prose-writing be free from the
measured cadence of the poetic line with
its varied unity of quantity, still, to be
artistic, it requires, in a remoter way, the
unitive balance of the sentence with the
harmonized subordination of its members.

The loftier the prose the more exacting in
its expression becomes this law, and in
those compositions, which are called prose-
poetry, language approaches closer and closer to metrical utterance; the less elevated
the theme of the prose-writer, the further
removed his work from the influence of this
law, until it comes down to the level of a
bare statement where there is and can be no
art.

Not only, however, is the rhythm of the
poetical measure a fulfillment of this fundamental law of art expression, but rhyme is
also an exemplification of its working.
Nothing appears more the result of chance
than rhyme, commonly regarded as a merely
arbitrary juxtaposition of similar syllabic
sounds at definite intervals concluding the
measure of the line. But rhyme, no less
than rhythm, is an external correspondence
with the law of unity in variety; for rhyme
is simply the regularly emphasized beat of
syllabic sounds, in whose similarity there is
a unison—supplying unity—with sufficient
difference to avoid identity, wherein we get
variety. Complete identity of sound in two

terminating syllables destroys rhyme, and so
does complete difference. It is in the combination of both that the music of ryhme is
found, and the delight we derive from it
arises, in truth, from that same esoteric law
of beauty, which ever demands expression in
variety governed by unity. Certain forms
of poetic conception find their only fitting
utterance in rhyme. Lyric poetry, of its
very nature, vehemently aspires to rhyme.
Its flight is only possible on the wings of
rhyme. It is only heroic verse which gathers
its strength from the transcendent sublimity
of an heroic theme, that can dispense with
rhyme, and then only by virtue of an intrinsic quality of self-elation, which lifts it high
into the empyrean, where it soars in perfect
balance like the king of birds above the
grosser atmosphere of clouds poised on
motionless wing in the serener spaces of the
heavens.

But rhyme is the exigency of lyric
poetry; for lyric poetry is the expression of
great and elevated passion transfused with
the glow of an illuminated imagination, and
this can only be satisfied with the music of

song. The law of beauty presses insistently
upon it, not only in the expression of rhythm
but in the demand for rhyme. And in this
we come to an aspect of this secret law which
reveals to us at the same time the sacrifice
of beauty in submitting to the obligations of
time and the transfiguration of the elements
of matter under the domination of that
higher law. Beauty, indeed, submits to the
yoke, for only by submission to time can her
word be made manifest ; but while she submits to temporal obligations, she only con-
cedes herself by exacting the fullest possible
response and by transfusing the sensible
media of her expression with her own higher
harmony. She exacts not only the cadent
music of the measured line, but the harmonized music of rhyme. The chariot of
harmony is drawn by the yoked steeds of
matter, submissive to her captive power, yet
transfigured by the glory of her presence.*
Rhyme is, therefore, not to be regarded

---

* "Cette magie du vers ne ressemble-t-elle pas aux plaintes
de la matière qui traine en frémissant le char de l'Harmonie,
déchirée sans doute, mais domptée, glorifiée, transfigurée par sa
puissance ?"—Ernest Hello, "L'Homme," Livre III., "La Convention, La Fantaisie et L'Ordre."

as a fortuitous concordance of chance syllables, but the organic manifestation of the
vital harmony of beauty under the imperative government of her secret law—unity
expressed by variety, and variety dominated
by unity.

Not only, however, does the law of
beauty govern in the world of creative art,
the world of the poet, but none the less in
the world of discriminative art, the realm
of criticism. Nothing has been more fatal
to the progress of art than the prevailing
notion that the critic is a man apart from
the artist. The critic who is not himself an
artist is not even a critic. To sit apart
and judge according to rule is simply to
put in motion the mechanism of convention.
None but an artist can understand the law
of beauty, and he who knows not the law
of beauty has no understanding of the
science of art; for what is criticism but
the judgment of the truth of art-work, and
how will the critic be able to appreciate
that truth who knows not its science, and
how will he comprehend its science who
does not understand the law of beauty ?

What other is the critic than the conscience of art,* and what is conscience but the judgment of the right or wrong of human works and deeds? It is a false and fatal distinction which would make the conscience a faculty apart from the intellect, a blind instinct, deflecting to the right or the left like the needle of the compass under the irresistible spell of some external power. The conscience is the intellect judging according to law, and the art conscience, which is criticism, is the intellect judging according to the law of beauty. The understanding of that law must include the appreciation of the imagination's supreme function in the sensible manifestation of the splendor of the idea. The art-critic, no less than the art-maker, should have a great imagination sympathetic with the intellectual word, sensitive to its faintest radiance, aglow with its splendors. If he have not the creative power, he must at least possess an equivalent power of comprehension. To comprehend is to equal, says Raphael, and a compre-

---

* "La Critique est la Conscience de L'Art."—Ernest Hello: "L'Homme," "L'Art."

hensive admiration lifts the soul to the superior level of the thing admired, and there can be no judgment save from the heights. Therefore must the critic, if he have not the creative faculty, possess the power of an equivalent admiration by which he ascends to that coigne of vantage, whence he may deliver judgment; for judgment may not come from the low levels of the valleys, but from the mountain-tops.

The first duty of the critic, I call it a duty since his deliverance is a function of conscience, is to discover and proclaim the beautiful. "Here is beauty," he cries aloud to the world. "Here is the splendor of truth; here is one whose utterance, according to the law of beauty, manifests the visible glory of the invisible word. Come ye and worship and be exalted in that glory and be made anew, pilgrims in the vale of time, whose souls are athirst for the living fountains of water; lift your faces to the brief illumination from the regions of supernal light that you may be refreshed and made strong." He is the watcher upon the tower to proclaim the glory of the dawn to the sleepers in the shrouded valley below. His voice should be the harbinger of good tidings, the assurance of hope, the confirmation of faith. This is his first duty; this is his last responsibility; and to be all this, he must himself be an artist whose power of comprehensive admiration must equal the power of creation, the seer and the herald of whose beauty he is to the peoples, who await the word of his judgment.

His office is positive, not negative; his mission not to destroy but to discover : not fault-finder, but path-finder should he be. Misfortune, indeed, is it that to him has been assigned by public misconception in these later days, the task of finding the flaw, of pulling down, until to criticise has become popularly synonymous with to destroy. But the just office of the critic is not to detect the flaw for destruction's sake, but for beauty's defense. The negative duty of destruction in his office comes only by virtue of the positive obligation of preservation. He is first, and foremost, a teacher of the science of the beautiful. If, in the exercise of his functions, it be not his office to give concrete expression to the law of beauty by creative power, it belongs to him to enunciate it and build up the structure of its science, point out and illustrate its principles, demonstrate its conclusions and then, after its positive establishment, like the sentinel upon the frontier, guard the kingdom of beauty from the inroad and assault of the enemy. It is only the destroyer he should destroy, only the invader he should slay, and then only in defense of the integrity of his precious charge.

It is in great part because the conception of the positive character of the critic has been lost in later times that we find the regions of art so widely laid waste at the end of our century. Instead of being the guardian of the treasures of the king, the critic has, in large measure, become himself a predatory robber, whose one object is to assault and kill. Instead of a steadfast, resolute defense, he has opened the gates to the foe, and in this failure of his trust, losing sight of the real end of his office, he would set up an usurpation in the midst of the kingdom he has betrayed, and grasp the

scepter it should be his noblest dignity to
defend; refusing to acknowledge or forgetting the law of beauty, he fails to understand
its science, and without knowledge of its
science, he can have no power of judgment,
and lacking judgment, he is bereft of conscience, and without conscience how can he,
in any sense of the word, be critic ?

We have but to look around us and see
the ravages in the realm of art, which have
followed upon this betrayal. The forces of
Agnosticism have broken into the sacred
precincts, and, like Timour, built its monument of skulls in the very sanctuary of art.
Realism is enthroned in the palace of beauty.
Art ceases to be the sensible expression of the
splendor of truth and becomes the loathsome
exhibition of the squalor of ugliness. Behold
the Nemesis of the critic's treason ! Men fall
down and worship ugliness, and call their
act of debasement Realism ! Where before
was art, Agnosticism has thrust its opposite,
and this it does, shameful parody of the
sacred word, in the name of truth ! Faithful
to its negative office of destruction, Realism—
the art-parody begotten by Agnosticism—the

foul monster of a hideous womb, even as
death is born of sin,—Realism thrusts upon
us its picture of failure and death. Is not
the world, it declares, in reality a mere
plexus of blind forces, crushing out life to
give life, giving life to destroy it? See
humanity, a beast groveling in its filthy den.
Nature is the author of disease and death.
This is reality. Let us realize the horror of
it as it is. Nature tells us of no God. Man
is born in the wrath of nature, lives the
victim of misfortune and disease and goes
down to hopeless corruption. Paint him in
the loathsome details of his real existence;
let us not deceive ourselves by the glamour
of the imagination, but let us give an exact
copy of man and nature as the one lives and
the other is, if we would know the truth,
harsh and ugly though it be.

All this Realism proclaims in the name
of a godless science. It is the assumption
and description of a godless nature and a
godless man, and it destroys art. It is a
false assumption and a false description.
It is the description of that which is not
true, of the unreal, for neither nature nor

man is without God.   It is the true that
is real; the most true, the most real; therefore God.   Nature and man are most true,
and therefore most real, when they most
faithfully reflect the Divine Truth, and most
beautiful when they most perfectly express
the splendor of that Divine Truth.   To paint
nature as ravenous with tooth and claw,
and man as simply bestial, is the satanic
view.   It is the doctrine that in deformity
is virtue, that in sin is order.   There is a
deformity in man's nature, that is, a disorder; for man has fallen from the ideal
and with him dragged down nature from
that perfect state, which is his true estate
Realism has abandoned God, and therefore
describes nature and man as abandoned by
God; but in spite of sin God has abandoned
neither.   Sin destroyed that order which
once united man and nature, through man,
in perfect harmony with his Creator; but
God, Whose Wisdom is perfect and Whose
Will is indefectible, vanquishes that disorder
by the introduction of a superior order,
overcomes the ravages of sin by converting
its penalties into an atonement by virtue of

a superior merit, and repairs the defect in
the natural order by an infinite reparation
in the supernatural order.   Human nature
is restored to its first perfection and dignity
and elevated to divinity in its assumption
by Jesus Christ.   The disorder of sin is
overcome by the voluntary acceptance of its
penalty in the divine satisfaction of the
Cross.   In Him, by Whom the wound in
man and nature was healed, is the fullness
of truth and beauty.   In Him, Who is the
the Way, the Truth and the Life, is the
fullness of reality.   He is at once the real
and the ideal, the real in the ideal and the
ideal in the real—the real in His own incom-
parable perfection ; the ideal as the perfect
model for all men.   It is only when men
fall away from this ideally real that they
become deformed and ugly.   It is upon this
failure that Realism has fixed its eyes.
It strives to depict with hideous exactness
the unreal man, the ugly man.   Based upon
the agnostic science, which fails to see in
Him the light of the world, it is equally
blinded to beauty.

Art teaches us to look at nature ideal-

ized, at nature as it was once in reality
when it corresponded in its primeval perfection to its Maker's plan. It seeks to
picture nature to us in that order which
made it beautiful when it was in reality the
cosmos. It depicts nature in truth, not in
falsehood ; in beauty, not in deformity. It
pictures the earth, not bringing forth thorns
and thistles, but "the fruit-tree yielding
fruit after its own kind," when the lion and
the lamb lay down together and God saw
that it was good. "And the Lord God had
planted a Paradise of pleasure from the
beginning, wherein He placed man whom
He had formed." This is not nature in
deformity, this is not nature corrupted, but
nature in truth—in reality. Art depicts man,
not crippled and maimed, but upright and
straight-limbed, not gross and foul, but pure
and clean ; not abased and corrupted, but
ennobled and chaste; not weak and vitiated,
but strong and virtuous. It depicts man as
he was in the beginning, the undefiled
image of his Maker, as he should be in
truth and in reality.

SYNTHESIS.

We have now approached our subject by three various roads. We first took an historical outline survey in the light of that first general principle of all of man's art-work, the relation of man to that something outside and beyond himself. We traced the leaven of this principle in the literature of the world, and we saw how the historical periods of literature ebbed and flowed under the domination of the law of that principle, like the tides of the ocean under the draw of the moon. The foundation of all the great art-work and literature of man we saw to be based on man's conception of, first, his relation to God, and through this to his brother-man. According to the intensity of man's conviction of the truth of this prime relation waxed and waned the greatness of his literature.

The conception of this primal relation

we called the science of man, using the word in its fullest and completest sense as the sum and conclusion of all of man's knowledge of himself and his destiny.

In our second lecture, we saw how the character of man's literature was drawn from the nature of his science; how, as he thought, so he lived and so he spoke. We dwelt on the phases of his conception of that primal relation which makes the eternal foundation of his science, his art and his literature, and we saw that in four ways only had he expressed that relation, namely, in Paganism, in Rationalism, in Pantheism and in Christianity, and that when he denied that relation in his skepticism or agnosticism immediately there began to follow a degeneration of his art and his literature.

Having gained this insight into the dependence of man's art and literature upon his science, our next consideration was to trace the nexus between his art and his science by explicating the meaning of art. In this analysis we established the correspondence between man's intellect and imagination, out of which arises the supreme law of art—the manifestation of unity by variety. The visible universe we saw to be the theater of that manifestation in space and in time. The intellect comprehends this unity, the imagination varies it, but always in accordance with the objective laws of space and time, so that the sensible expression of beauty, which constitutes art, falls necessarily and helpfully within the domain of order. Criticism we saw to be the positive duty of protecting that domain from violation, and that when criticism loses the conception of its proper office and degenerates into the negative function of destruction, it opens the way to the Realism, which usurps the throne of art and destroys beauty; since it is the aim of art to picture man in his perfection, man in the ideal, not man fallen away from that ideal and in the deformity which sin has wrought within him.

In such wise have we approached the summit of our subject from three various roads, whose prospects as we moved upward and onward, have grown wider and profounder with the progress of our ascent.

Our aim has been to get at the reasons of literature and to arrive at the final ideal of what literature ought to be, for this I conceive to be, in truth, the philosophy of literature. It now devolves upon us to retrace our steps and, once more, climb the precipitous sides of this mountain of philosophical research by still another path, whence we may gain an even wider and profounder prospect than we have yet enjoyed, and at the termination of which we may hope to reach the summit of summits, from whose height all the views which we have hitherto gained may melt into the unbroken prospect of one complete and glorious whole.

Let us go back to the remotest past, back to antiquity as it lies in the distant morning-land of human tradition, to find our proper and prime starting-point. At the same time let us remember that by antiquity we do not mean either the old or the ancient; the old is that which has wasted away under the solvent breath of time, and the ancient that which indeed remains, but in the inanimate forms of the past fixed in death, reminding us of the life that once was by pointing the painful moral to its transience. The old is decrepit and infirm, the ancient intact, but lifeless. Antiquity is neither of these; the finger of age has never touched it; the flight of centuries has never chilled its spirit; for antiquity has become the imperishable memory, perennial in the human soul, of that prime season of man's existence in the morning of life, when he walked conversant with his Maker, and nature, through man's free obedience to the Divine Will, was harmonious with the human word. Antiquity still lives in the universal tradition of the Golden Age amongst all peoples at all times. The religious books of all peoples recount it ; it runs like an underground current at the roots of their lives and their history ; it pervades their philosophies, is the minor chord of their songs and the measure of their tragedies; it is always and sharply attested by that sense of sin and guilt which has weighed upon all peoples from the beginning. It is the root of the world's religions, seeking some way of propitiating an offended Divinity for the sin committed and of wiping out the stain contracted. Skepticism has never been able to eradicate it, nor Agnosticism to obscure it. It is grafted forever in the impotence of fallen human nature, and that radical impotence is ever openly confessing itself in the sin, the crime and the misery of humanity under the unclosed eye of the revolving sun and beneath the sleepless watch of the lidless stars. The knowledge of his present weakness is the perpetual witness of man's primal power, and the sense of his unceasing misery the constant reminder of his past felicity. The voice of the tradition of the golden prime of his first day, lived in the happiness of the perfect accord of the human with the Divine Will and amidst the serene concord of nature in the solemn gladness of a glorious peace, finds its constant echo in the dimmed chambers of the human soul, longing for that pristine harmony which the primal sin lost for all the sons of Adam.

Antiquity is the freshness of this memory in the soul of man before he had strayed far from the sight of the gates of Eden; when the living converse of his Maker yet lingered in his ear and he sighed for that large knowledge which sin had obscured in his intellect; when he still fed his heart upon the lost sweetness of that perfect love which sin had poisoned into concupiscence; when knowledge was higher than science, when order had not yet felt the wound of the creature's rebellion and nature was still divinely linked with grace through the lofty freedom of the submission of the unimpaired human will. Then was the holy season of that paradisial innocence, which was wisdom, and the perfect hour of creation's unbroken music, which was order, when God saw that all was good, and man's soul dwelt in the illumination of his Maker's countenance, knowing the good, not by the tedious process of an enfeebled and darkened intellect groping painfully from truth to truth, but in the expansive light of the Divine Word graciously audible through all the regions of his primal happiness.

It is in the cradle lands of the race, in the Orient, that this reminiscence lingered freshest, where man has ever lain prostrate under the awful sense of his tremendous

loss. There he still lives, dazed as it were
by the catastrophe of his fall. There the
sense of his ruin has weighted his soul,
relieved only by the faded memory of his
lost high estate. There he spurns earth and
seeks to escape from the discord of evanescent
nature by fixing his mind upon the abstract
contemplation of things apart from space and
time. There he turns from the slow processes of science and seeks knowledge by
intuition. It is not in the paltry details of
the workings of matter that he seeks his
knowledge, but, striving to transcend the
heavy bondage of the body, he would soar on
the filmy wings of contemplation to the
regions of light and dwell naked in the
brilliant heart of their mysteries. There he
knows not the painful science of conclusions ;
to him all true knowledge is of intuition, and
this gained only by exaltation of the soul
above the constraining limits of the despised
senses. The tradition of Eden, which sur-
vives in his memory confused and dimmed,
he would make the living present, and forgetting the consequent disorder and infirmity of
his own powers as well as the eclipse of

grace in his darkened soul, he would, in his
impotence, hear the sound of the Divine
Voice again and dwell in the light of the
Divine Countenance as he once dwelt in the
perfect morning of his life. In the Orient,
man is a mystic, fixing his constrained sight
on the vague and vast image of the distant
prime which glimmers confusedly in his
blurred memory. So he scorns the things
of earth and time and dwells in the immensities of contemplation and would leap by the
flash of intuition into the perfection of all
knowledge and the possession of all beauty.

The spirit of the Orient is contemplation.* With the restless activity of the
Occident, battling step by step through
devious ways to the knowledge of conclusions, it has no sympathy. It seeks the
supreme repose of intuition.

Men migrated westward from the cradle
lands of the race, and as they moved onward,
the gates of Eden faded from sight. The
tradition of the golden prime went with them,
but assumed other shapes and was clothed

---

* "L'Esprit de l'Orient c'est l'Art, c'est-à-dire la contemplation, c'est-à-dire le repos."—Hello.

in other forms. Settling in the garden-regions around the blue Mediterranean, far from the hallowed land where the race was created in the lap of grace, under new conditions and less sublime associations they lost the haunting memory of the Divine Presence on earth and fashioned its lingering echoes into the fables of humanized gods. With the Greeks, Divinity was degraded to the condition of fallen humanity. Not the knowledge of the Supremely Divine constituted the science of Greece, but the knowledge of human things. The spirit of Greece was human science—the science that labors from premise to conclusion. "Greece," says Hello, "does not contemplate; she judges, compares and measures."* Greece has no theology; she has only a philosophy, and this philosophy is simply an intellectual measurement of natural and human things. The Divine is beyond her compass, for the Divine is immeasurable, and Greece possesses only a human measure by which she gauges

---

* "L'Esprit de la Grèce c'est la science, c'est-à-dire le travail. La Grèce ne contemple pas; elle juge, elle compare, elle mesure."—Hello.

human proportions. She knows only that which comes within the measure of human reason, and the highest law of her science is the due proportions of the works of the human mind. The law of her art is the proportion between parts. Her architecture and her sculpture begin and end in the proportion of lines. Her drama is her sculpture in motion. Her language and her literature are models of balance and proportion. Her statues are models of the perfection of the proportions of the human form. Her temples do not speak the sublimity of Divinity, but the sense of proportion in humanity. She understands the law of order only in its natural application. The higher order of the supernatural she knows not. Beyond the natural ordering of the visible world she saw only Fate—an indefinite vastness encompassing the universe, not by a superior law that could draw order out of disorder, but by an inexorable necessity that drove and crushed with a blind force. Though she retained the tradition of the Golden Age, Greece had lost the memory of its supernatural character; she possessed only the labored knowledge of conclusions: hers was the spirit of human science only.

In time, the spirit of science becomes the formula; its life congeals into the hard and fast lines of the rule, the formulated law in which the sap of life is dried out. Rome is this formula and she devours Greece—the spirit of science—as she had devoured Carthage—the spirit of cunning.* Greece had become a cadaver before she became a victim of the Roman wolf. The spirit of her science had fled and the wolf fed not upon the living body, but upon the corrupted carcass. Rome had been nourished at the breast of a wolf and the blood of a wolf was in her veins. As the nations of the ancient world around her fell into corruptions and death, she devoured them and absorbed them, but she did not change them, nor did she revivify them. She ruled them by their own formulæ—the dead letter of their ancient life. In the land of the Pharaohs, she became Egyptian; in Palestine, Jewish; in Hellas,

---

* "Le jour où Rome dévora la Grèce, la formule dévora la science. Aussi, certainement que l'Orient est spéculatif et que la Grèce est scientifique, Rome est formulaire."
—Hello.

Grecian. She became all these and all these were in death. To them she gave not her own life, and to her they imparted the seeds of death. Into her pantheon she received all their gods, worshipped at all their fanes, sacrificed at all their altars, partook of their corruption and their license and their error, and fed herself to repletion on their putrescence. She was all things to all peoples in death. She had no power of re-creation; old age was upon them and she could not rejuvenate them; they were dying out of the world and she could not save them. She could only dominate them by the power of her arms and govern them by the force of the formula. To her, law, not as a living spirit fashioning, developing, vivifying, but law, the fixed rule, the mechanical formula, crushing as it measured, was the supreme power, and that law was martial Rome, Rome of the iron legions, within whose hand the dying nations were clenched as in the vice of a huge machine. The Roman ruler is a soldier; the emperor is simply imperator. He governs by martial discipline, by force of the formula. All her virtue is in her armies—human machines moved by the power of the formula.

The Roman statue is that of a soldier; the Greek statue is that of the perfect human form. The Roman statue expressed the force of law, the Greek expressed the fullness of human beauty. The statue of the Orient is neither military nor human; it is a symbol; it is huge, it is monstrous, enigmatical. It strives to express a mystery that finds no adequate medium of manifestation in the work of human hands. It is the sphinx dreaming of eternity, but speechless, because the Orient, though dwelling in the reminiscence of Eden, has forgotten the language in which Adam conversed with his Maker. Or, it is the statue of Memnon, musical for the moment when smitten by the first ray of the morning sun, as if in memory of that first golden dawn of human integrity, and then mute, as if with the oppression of some mysterious catastrophe, Titanic stone, misshapen, silent amid the waste lands of its eternal deserts.

Greece had no dreams of eternity. Her life was human, consummated within the

bounds of human time.   She had no mystery
but Fate, and this she concealed with flowers.
Human science and human beauty were the
goals of her striving.   Rome   knew   only
Rome, and for her, Rome was the world.
Rome universal, the Rome of the twelve
tables, Rome the formula.

In the Orient, humanity was nothing ;
earth, with all the things of time and space,
was spurned for the dream of that infinite
substance in whose mysterious embrace the
evanescent world lies.   In Greece, humanity
was everything ; the mystery beyond was
hidden in the eyeless fate from which man
turned to study man. At Rome, both mystery
and humanity disappeared in the formula;
to the Roman Rome was all : religion was
Rome, humanity was Rome, and Rome was
the soldier ruling the world by the formula.
In the Orient, man, the finite, is lost in the
abyss of the infinite ; in Greece, the infinite
is forgotten in the activity of the finite ; in
Rome, both are canceled in the sterility of
the formula.   Beauty, in the Orient, is in
the dream of the infinite ; all its art is in the
symbol.   In Greece, beauty is in the perfect

form of humanity, all its art is in the expression of the perfection of human proportions. Beauty is not known at Rome at all ; Rome has no art ; she imports it.   She enjoins upon the seamen, who transport the statues of Greece across the seas to the Roman capitol, the command to replace those that may be broken on the way by replicas. She believes in the infallible virtue of the formula.   Her literature is made according to the measure of Greek models.   Cicero, Virgil and Horace write Greek in Latin. Roman literature is rhetoric and imitation. The application of the formula was her true function, and the formula is applied by force.   At Rome, vir is the strong man, the soldier, and the strength of the soldier is virtue.

In the Orient human life dreams itself away and petrifies in immobility. In Greece, it exhausts itself and putrifies in excessive movement.   At Rome, it cracks and crumbles away like some vast machine worn out.

In Asia, in Greece and in Rome, the ancient world exhausts itself. Old age is

upon it, and dissolution approaches fast.
The fullness of time has come.*

We said that art was the sensible expression of the beautiful, and that beauty is
the splendor of truth.   We considered the
relations of the imagination and the intellect
in art, their interdependence and the laws
governing art expression arising out of that
relation, as well as the relation of both to
the objective order of the world in space
and time ; and we established the universal
law of all art expression to be unity manifested in variety and variety bound by unity.
We also pointed out the dependence of
man's art in literature upon his conception
of himself in his relation to the Divine,
upon his science, using this term in its
completest sense.   Let us look at the ancient
world, summed up in Asia, Greece and Rome,
in the light of our doctrine.

In the Orient, all man's science was
concentrated in the effort to contemplate

---

* In the third section of the work entitled "L'Homme," in
the chapter devoted to the subject of Art, Hello sublimely
develops this tremendous contrast between the Orient, Greece
and Rome. It is one of the most striking pictures in literature.

primal truth face to face in its naked glory,
untempered by moment of time or point of
space. The open eye of the human intellect
sought to gaze upon the consuming splendors
of infinite substance, even as the Infinite
contemplates Himself. Time and space in
Oriental thought were delusive phantasms
grossly concealing eternal mind. Nature did
not manifest but obscured the thought of
the infinite. Matter and man were evanescent shadows forever melting away into the
abyss of nothingness : to escape from the
delusions of earthly existence and to be
absorbed by infinite substance is the goal
of all striving. The science of the Orient
was a subjective pantheism. Its art and its
literature were fashioned out of its science.
Its art and its literature are symbolic, vast,
vague, indefinite and grotesque suggestions
of the infinite dream, which the Orient was
impotent to express and could only hope-
lessly shadow. The intellect of the Orient
was swallowed up in the contemplation of
an absolute unity. *It knew no variety.* To it,
space and time were unrealities : it failed
to understand their laws and was blind to

the endless variety of their manifestations.
It never understood the fundamental law of
art, unity expressed by variety and variety
bound by unity.   It formulated its science
into absolute unity; it sought its life in
the arid heights of pure abstraction.   With
it there was no sensible splendor, because
it ignored variety; and because it ignored
variety, it gave no expression to beauty.
With it was no true art, no true literature.   It developed immense systems of
speculation, which it sometimes fashioned
into verse and epic, but these were metaphysical discourses beyond the limits of
human living, scorching and drying up the
fountains of the imagination.   Its monuments, its temples, its writings were gigantic
symbols, inarticulate witnesses of man's
vain attempt to utter the infinite in human
speech.   The Orient has no history; it has
been petrified for forty centuries; it has left
us the sphinx, the pyramids and hiero-
glyphics.

In Greece man had turned his back
upon the dream of the Orient. The legend
of the Golden Age persisted in his fable,

but it was thrust into the background of his existence, while the Orient still stood beating on the closed gates of Eden for entrance into the garden of delight. Greece garlanded the primal legend with the flowers of a graceful imagination. In Hellas, the tradition had dropped out of man's life, though it lingered in his memory. From the awful shadow of the infinite, he turned to the radiant though brief hours of humanity. Life was a banquet glowing with all the offerings of time and space. Death had no meaning to him, though he might fear it. He only asked to die among the flowers. The all of existence was within the span between the cradle and the grave. He busied all the powers of mind and body with human affairs. All his science was human; his philosophy, his literature and his art, his politics were keenly human. His religion was human, for his gods were only magnified human images mirrored in the gigantic forces of nature. His deities jostled each other in the human throng. Olympus was a Greek banquetting hall where immortal Greeks reclined human wise and sipped ambrosia, subject to the same human love, hates, hopes, fears and ambitions, as stirred the hearts of men at Athens.

In Greece, humanity was all : in the Orient, humanity was nothing. To the Greek, variety was the excellence of human life. Nature was but the various modes of man, seeing himself in the glory of sun and moon, in the breath of the zephyr, in the violence of the whirlwind, in the cerulean depths of the sea, in the azure of heaven, in the perfume and color of the flower, in the green and gold of the hills and the fields, in running waters and in flowing fountains. All nature was animate, instinct with reflected human movement ; Greece was human movement incessant—a movement that began and ended in humanity. Greece had lost sight of the eternal repose of infinite unity, as Asia had forgotten its manifestation in infinite variety. Greek art is human art, Greek literature is human literature ; both are conterminous, but neither escapes the confining bounds of the finite. It knew not sublimity, which is the breath of the infinite stirring in man's soul. It knew human science, but it knew no more. It was forever seeking a change, resting nowhere, moving everywhere. Variety was the law of its restless life, and in variety it exhausts itself. Its dissolution comes through excessive movement. It divided and sub-divided itself, faction against faction, sophist against sophist, school against school. It had lost all conception of the higher life of the Divine Unity, and therefore perished. When its own life became simply the activity of the parasite in the cadaver, it was prepared for Rome, and the Roman wolf devoured it.

Greece conquered the Orient the day that Troy was taken, and that day Rome was born. With Æneas the Orient came to Latium, but Anchises did not come with Æneas; the dream of the golden dawn remained in the East. Rome forgot it, or rather she transformed it into the dream of universal dominion. What the Orient had spurned as the fleeting shadows of unreality, Rome put forth all her energies to conquer— time and space, a dominion enduring through all time and through all space. She would conquer by force of armies, she would hold by force of law. As the nations about her

grew old, she brought them under her yoke;
as their spirit had perished she ruled them
by their own formula. It was not her wisdom that dictated this policy but her
instinct—the mechanical instinct of the
people that lived by rule alone. In her
eyes, conquered peoples were machines to be
run according to the rule of their own na-
tures, that they might thus diversely grind
common grist for the Roman mill. In this
wise Rome increased in bulk by accretions ;
she did not grow by virtue of any principle
of organic life. Although her dominion
became conterminous with the known world,
the world did not become Roman. The
various peoples, subject to her, remained
what they had been—Greek, Egyptian, Jewish, Roman, Macedonian. Rome only
sought to rule them each after its own kind
by its own formula. She conquered and
held a dead world by submitting to the law
of its death. The day was to come when she
would not die, but break to pieces.

The Orient never understood the supreme
law of art. Its life was absorbed in impossibly

straining after an absolute unity, which disdained expression in the varieties of time and space. The necessities of unity crushed out the possible freedom of variety in the Oriental mind. So immense was its dream of the infinite that time could not encompass it, so vast was its phantasm that space could not hold it. Not understanding the fullness of the supreme law of art, it could not create an adequate form to express itself; it symbolized itself in hugeness and monstrosities. Its literature was a vast dream full of the phantasmagoria of sleep, as vague and as monstrous as its statues and its temples. In its dream of absolute unity it forgot the infinite power of expression in variety. Its unity became a pantheism wherein all differences were unreal and unsubstantial.

Greece never understood the fullness of the supreme law of art. Turning its eyes upon the multitudinous variety in the life of man and activity of nature, it lost sight of that invisible unity of which man and nature are but the visible expression in variety. It lost itself in the mazes of the labyrinth of nature and of man. It gave itself up to the excesses of variety without the constraining bond of unity. Variety grew into license and freedom was ground to dust under its incessant attrition. Its art became multitudinous, its literature voluminous; it created much, it conserved nothing. Finally, after the day of Alexander, it descended to the minutiæ of imitation, and at the same time, bred the ephemera of the rhetorician who made the living art of writing a set of dead rules. Greece was growing putrescent—was being prepared for the wolf.

Rome neither understood variety nor unity, but it did understand the mechanism of both; it carried from the Orient the vast shadow of unity, which it crystallized in the formula of Rome's universal domination. The mechanism of variety it learned in the Occident whither it had emigrated. In itself it found the formula of unity, and in the numerous peoples with which it came in contact in the Western world, it discovered the formulæ of variety. What it believed in was the formula, but neither in unity nor in variety. The living law, which is the order of the organic life, Rome could not understand. The dead rule—the mechanical order of a dead world—it understood well, and upon it built the vast bulk of its mechanical existence. Its art and its literature were constructed on the principles of mechanics. It saw the Greek models and imitated the Greek formulæ.

Neither in the Orient, nor in Greece, nor in Rome do we find the living fullness of art and literature. For none of these understood the supreme law of art : unity in variety, and variety in unity, expressed by the Living Word. The Orient knew unity, but it did not understand variety ; Greece knew variety, but it did not comprehend unity ; Rome understood the formulæ of both, but conceived not their living spirit. When Rome ruled the earth by the power of the formula, the fullness of time had come.

Where, then, will be found the ideal art and the ideal literature ? The art and the literature, which are the living expression of the fullness of the Divine Word and at the same time comprehend unity and express variety, fulfilling the supreme law of art ; the literature, which comprehends unity without forgetting variety, and understands variety without neglecting unity ?

When the fullness of time had come, there was born One, at whose birth the angels sang, "Hosanna in the Highest, and peace on earth to men of good will," and to whose crib the mysterious Orient sent its wise men, guided by a star in the heavens, to offer their gifts and adore Him at whose coming the gates of Eden were to re-open. He went about preaching a new doctrine in an old world. The life of the nations had departed. Rome moved the world by the power of her colossal machinery; the world moved, but it did not live. The vital powers were exhausted. The world was ancient and worn out. The law of Moses was observed in the letter, not in the spirit. Rome spoke in Pilate—and with Rome spoke the ancient world—when, shrugging his shoulders, the Roman Governor asked the silent and macerated Prisoner before his tribunal, "What is truth?" And then, turning, washed his hands and delivered up the innocent One to die the death according to the Jewish formula.

The ancient world looked upon the face of the Living Truth and knew Him not. Rome knew only the formula, and to the death, by power of the formula, betrayed the Living Truth. And from that death the Living Truth rose, and the ancient world, dead in the sin of Adam, was conquered and regenerated. It was raised like Lazarus putrescent in the grave, to life again.

In Him, who died the death by the formula sanctioned by Rome, and who renewed the life of the world, was the fullness of eternity and the consummation of time. It is He who said, "I am the way, the truth and the life." He is the life in truth of which the Orient dreamed, the fullness of eternal life, the unchanging, everlasting life in which there is no shadow of turning, the sum of all life, the Alpha and Omega of all existence, the infinite and the absolute Being of the uncommunicable name mysteriously spoken to Moses out of the burning bush : "I Am Who Am." When men questioned Him, His answer was, "Before Abraham was, I Am." The gray-haired wisdom of the East, mysteriously guided to His cradle, came to acknowledge Him. Here was the new life of the old world, the living power of the dead peoples, the infinite life of which the Orient dreamed but knew not, the infinite unity which has begotten all things in endless variety.

He is the Truth ; the Truth, which Greece sought in vain in the ever-shifting and changing play of human existence, the Truth, which its philosophy impotently guessed at, the Truth, to which its science could not reason, the Truth, which it could not find in the lights and shadows of the evanescent forms of nature, the Truth it sought in the vicissitudes of matter, but which it had really banished behind the flowered mask of the Fate that in ignorance it feared and upon whose unchangeable countenance it dared not look. It searched all time and space for the Truth, but found only the endless mutability of finite existence ; and restless with its perpetual searching, it threw itself into the arms of chance and with Epicurus delivered itself up to the fading pleasure of the melting moment, or with Zeno gazed despairingly into the hollow eyes of the mask which it had fastened before the face of the Truth it did not understand. But the Truth, which Greece found not, is in Him by whom were made all things and without whom was made nothing that was made. Greek reveled in the works of His hands, but knew Him not. In the works of His hands it sought the fullness of knowledge, but found it not. For in Him alone is the fullness of knowledge, the power of the unity of science, the virtue of the unity of life, which makes variety one and which makes unity various.

He is the way, the living law of life, which Rome had mechanized into the despotism of the formula. The ancient peoples were bowed under an iron yoke, but the formula was not the way of life to freedom. It was not the living power; it was simply a mechanical force. It was not a law, it was a rule. It did not guide men by a superior light; it dominated them by a blind force. It might preserve peace by the suppression of external disorder; it could not make peace by the creation of an interior order. But the living law is organic, it is the order of life, the fulfillment and perfection of being. It is the way of the living Truth, and Jesus Christ was Truth eternal and Life eternal. The mission of the formula was the universal rule of the dead world ; the mission of the law of Jesus Christ is the universal regeneration of the new world by the way of eternal life.

He came to give eternal life and fulfill the dream of the Orient ; to bestow the fullness of knowledge and perfect the science of Greece ; to replace the universal formula with the universal law of living righteousness ; to destroy the formulæ of the nations which invidiously distinguished between Jew and Gentile, Greek and Roman, bondman and free, by making all men one with Himself who is One with the Eternal Father. He established a Kingdom on earth in this world, though not of it. That Kingdom is Christendom. By an abyss as deep and wide as death is this Kingdom of Christ separated from the ancient world. By as much as its life is profoundly deeper, vaster and higher than the ancient life, by so much is the literature of Christendom

profoundly deeper, vaster and higher than
the literature of the ancients. It is rich in
all the mystery and sublimity of the Orient
without its obscurity and the gloomy shadows
of its symbols. It is more various and
wider than that of the Greeks; yet one in
all its infinite variety. It is more universal
than Rome, and at the same time what
Rome never was, living and perennial, vital
and organic, governed by the living law and
living by the law which governs it. It is
of all peoples, yet more than any people.
It is Greek, Roman, French, Italian, English, Spanish, German or American. It is
as various as these, variously one with the
life of each and at the same time living
with a spirit more than all. Its spirit is
one and universal, its manifestations many
and various. What literature is comparable with the literature of Christendom?
In theology, in philosophy, in epic and in
lyric, in drama and in history, none is so
various, none so profound, none so sublime,
none so universal. Nowhere has the human
word found wider, deeper, sublimer and completer expression. It is all this because it is

instinct with a life more than human, because it is the Divine Word dwelling in the minds and hearts of men, the Divine Word with the fullness of eternal life impregnating and supernaturalizing the human word. It is Christ dwelling amongst us, regenerating human life and regenerating the human word.

The Divine Word the Orient knew not, Greece knew not, Rome knew not.

What was this power of regeneration? It was the eternal Word of God, revealing the Father to man and in that manifestation revealing man to himself. The ancient world knew not God as he is, and therefore knew not man as he is. The light of the living Word made flesh has manifested to us what was hidden from the wisdom of the ancients. We are not our own; we are bought with a price; our bodies are God's temples, and the joy and terror of life depends upon our keeping these temples pure or in defiling them. Here is a new conception of life, a new dignity, for in it the things of time become freighted with the awful interests of eternity. By the power of that Divine Word

the old world has become other ; human existence has taken on a new meaning ; time
is vested with the power of eternity, and
earth becomes the vestibule of Heaven. In
the Orient time and space were nothing ; at
Athens and at Rome, time and space were
everything and eternity nothing. In Christendom time and space are the grace of a
wonderful probation whose term is the fullness of eternal life. And this eternal life
dependent upon the right using of this temporal probation is equally within the power
of the lowest and the highest. The eternal
seal of this regenerating power of the Divine
Word is impressed alike upon every human
soul, and in its redeeming power Cæsar's
slave is as great as Cæsar himself. Here
time is encompassed and surcharged with the
fullness of eternity ; the value of a single soul
becomes greater than the wealth of all the
nations, its dignity more than the majesty
of empires. By the power of this Divine
Word, the horizon of human life has expanded to the plenitudes of eternity. Man exists
in time, but lives in eternity.

Out of the new life of Christendom has

grown the literature of Christendom, a life beyond the possible conception of the ancient world, and a literature beyond its utterance. Its principle of vitality is that we are not our own; we are bought with a price; our bodies are the temples of the Holy Ghost.

From this root has grown the literature of Christendom. The Greek drama, which was the completest dramatic expression of the ancient world, dealt with statuesque situations; it arranged into prolonged scenes fixed attitudes of magnified human passions and sufferings, grouped under the domination of an implacable power, blindly and irresistibly determining the inevitable catastrophe.* The drama of Christendom is a development of action and character, working out from the premise of the free choice of the deliberate human will to its culminating act in happiness or misery. Mark the vast difference, the Greek dramatist saw tragedy only in Fate, externally determining human destiny. He never understood that we are temples of the Holy Ghost and that the meaning of life lies in our keeping those

---

* See De Quincy's "Theory of Greek Tragedy."

temples clean, or in defiling them. The
Christian dramatist finds the whole meaning
of life in the purity or in the defilement of
these temples, and with him, the drama of
life consists in the brief but eternal choice of
the human will fixing its immortal destiny
by its own human act in the light of supernatural law. The Greek measured the tragedy of life by the blind force of Fate. The
Christian measures it by the free power of
the human will in accepting or rejecting the
graces of redemption. We are bought with
a price, but we have the power of rejecting
the ransom by the treason of our wills. Here
is the unique and living principle of the
literature of Christendom. Upon this supernatural foundation it is forever built, and it
can never get away from it. Even the
attempt in recent literature to dislodge it
from those foundations, witnesses to its abid-
ing anchorage; for the literature of the
school which would reject the Christian
basis, gathers its sole interest from the force
of the Christian principles it would reject.*

---

* See Mallock's Dissertation on Positivist Literature, in his
work entitled: "Is Life Worth Living?"

While it would tear down the human temples of the Holy Ghost, its only interest in doing so turns upon the character of their sanctity. Were not this Christian conception of human life indelibly stamped and fixed in the social conscience of Christendom, the modern school of naturalism would have neither meaning nor occupation. It cannot escape the controlling presence of the ideal it would obliterate, and it has no articulate utterance save in the coin of the speech cast in the mints of Christian literature. To the Turk, the literature of naturalism can have no meaning. It is only understandable by virtue of Christian supernaturalism, and its ideals are only parodied images of the Christian idea mirrored into deformity by the oblique grossness of the reflecting medium. Out of the intense conception of the tremendous interests of human living, its vast reaching to eternity, the awful imports of all the details making up the catena of free acts that bind forever to the eternal result, has been woven the literature of Christendom. From the Christian promise of eternal life, measuring and fulfilling the sum of all the minutest acts of the human soul in its earthly probation, comes the principle of its unity, not only binding time and space into co-ordinate consistency, but linking them indissolubly with an eternal end. The penetrating light which the supernatural principle throws upon every minutest human action, searching the human conscience in its every judgment, illuminating every relation in the religious, social, domestic and civic life of man, throws its intense and exhaustive splendor over the whole field of man's existence, broken into colors and massed into innumerable lights and shades, prismed into variegated images by the multitudinous hopes, fears and passions of man, giving illimitable depth and perspective to the picture limned only by the profound background of the infinite. Here are the elements of its variety the field of whose unceasing play is from horizon to horizon of a celestial empyrean beyond and encompassing the narrow limits of time and space. Here human life is one by virtue of an organic unity radiating from the center, and at the same time pouring back from the circumference, of the infinite. Here human

life is profoundly various by virtue of the
infinitely multiplied manifestations of that
unity in the manifold relations of man's
life, charged with the multitudinous interests
of that eternal unity ceaselessly exhibiting
itself in the regions of time and space. Here
is given the principle of the supreme law of
art—the unity which manifests itself in variety, and the variety which is bound by
unity. The relation of the one to the many
and the many to the one, arising from the
very nature of their being, constitutes that
order which is the organic law of their government. Unity manifested by variety and
variety unfolding unity under the government of the supreme law of order, is the
essence of all art. In Christianity alone do
we find the fullness of the principle of that
law. In Christian art and in Christian
literature alone do we find the fullness of the
utterance of that law. For it is only in
Jesus Christ that we find the life, the truth
and the way; the Life which is Infinite and
One, the Truth which variously manifests in
the world of space and time the infinite
fecundity of that absolute and Eternal Life;

the Living Law, which, while it conserves
and unites, at the same time distinguishes
and keeps distinct the essences of all things
in the order of their various being by the
power of that Divine Word by which they
are. ''For in the beginning was the Word,
and the Word was with God and the Word
was God. Through Him were all things
made and without Him was made nothing
that was made; in Him was life, and the
life was the light of men.''

STYLE.

THE VARIETY OF THE FREEDOM OF THE WORD.

———•———

There remains one aspect of our subject-matter, which I have reserved for our final consideration, inasmuch as it deals with the philosophy of literature more especially in its outward manifestation, though, indeed, the principles which underlie it are as intimate as those which we have just been considering. We now come to ask ourselves what is style, or what is the same thing, what is the philosophy of style ? Anything so individual as style would seem to elude any attempt at analysis and definition ; in one sense this is true, for the individual is beyond the reach of genera and species, something all of itself, a subtle particularity sole and alone within the periphery of its own being, one of those ultimates which, though open to the apprehension, is completely shut out from the comprehension of the human intellect. We see it and recognize it, but we do not grasp it. All this is true if we seek to trace style down to the abysses of individuality; for that which is lowest in species is an ultimate upon which human thought must rest, just as much as that which is highest in genera or transcendent. On the heights the intellect can not go beyond being, and in the depths can not plumb farther than individuality. Though indeed style be something particular and individual, and in so much defies all analysis, we can trace it in the scale of things if we may not satisfactorily define it; and while we preserve due regard to its idiosyncracies, we can point its place within the regions of the universal law of art and literature.

It was given to man to speak; the brute is dumb. It was given to man to name all the creatures of the earth. His power of naming them is the sign of his dominion. Language belongs to the rational creature alone. He who understands and knows must have some mode of expressing his thought and his knowledge, that his nature may be fulfilled; for thought without speech is a power in darkness. The act of the rational power is thought, and speech is the outward expression of its activities. Understanding and knowledge seek diffusion ; they are communicative by their own nature. Speech is the exploitation of the rational nature. Did not the rational nature possess this capacity of self-expression, of communicating its activities and of receiving in kindred thought nourishment for its powers by the medium of speech, human reason would atrophy and man would fall back to the level of the brute. Language was given to him that he might conserve and perfect his rational powers ; the human word was bestowed upon man that he might make himself manifest.

Thought is the interior word of the mind, the image of reality mirrored in the power of the rational faculty, through which the soul looks out upon the universe and knows it. When this interior word corresponds to the reality of the universe, then may it be called the interior word of truth. In this power of conceiving and expressing truth resides the likeness of man to his Maker. Man was made to possess the truth, and in the possession of the truth to perfect himself in the divine image. The Eternal

Word, which is the intrinsic glory of the Divine Intellect, has extrinsically expressed that divine glory in creation. When the interior word of the human intellect faithfully images that external splendor of the Divine Word, then alone does it possess the truth. The power of the interior word was given to man that he might possess the truth; the power of the external word was given to man that he might express the truth of the interior word and, after the manner of the rational creature, manifest the glory of the Divine Word in the universe of creatures. It was given to man alone to tell of the glory of the works of the hand of his Creator.

Language is the human word, and style is the variety of the human word manifesting the glory of the interior word of truth. If the spoken word be not the faithful image of the interior word, it is a sham; if the interior word be not the faithful reflex of the glory of the external word of God spoken in the universe of creatures, it is a sham. Truth is the sole power of the human word. Not to speak truth is to obscure the external glory of the Creator, to vitiate order and to deny reason. Untruth obscures the external glory of the Creator by refusing to voice that which man was created to proclaim ; it vitiates order by denying the correspondence between the reality, which is, and the truth of the word, which ought to be; and it denies reason, when it denies the truth which is the life of reason. We have, therefore, a threefold relation; the truth of the word of the mouth, which depends upon its correspondence with the word of thought; the truth of the word of thought, which depends upon its correspondence with the truth of the universe ; and finally the truth of created things, which depends upon their correspondence with the Eternal Word of the Divine Intellect. Between the Eternal Word and the things of His making, there must ever be perfect correspondence, since they are only by His power and without Him was made nothing that was made. It is only in the interior word of man's thought and the spoken word that falsity can enter in. When that interior word fails to image the truth of things and the word of the mouth fails to express the truth of the interior

word, then is the human word perverted
from the service of Him who has designed
it to tell His own glory ; it becomes the
instrument of destruction in the service of
him who denied the glory of the Eternal
Word and affirmed the everlasting lie. "I
Am who Am " is the eternal affirmation of
the Eternal Word, the name of infinite life.
"I who am not, Am " is the cry of the
Satanic rebel, the proclamation of pride in
the creature, who would usurp the place of
his Creator.

The perfect human word was given to
man in the Garden of Eden, and its sole
office was to tell the glory of the perfect work
of the power of the Eternal Word. When
man fell the interior word lost that perfect
power of truth, which mirrored the unbroken
light of the truth of things in the crystalline
sphere of a perfected reason ; and the external word of man lost that power of perfect
expression which manifested the truth, the
order and the glory of creation, finding its
rational utterance in human speech. Since
that time has the word of thought been
obscured and human utterance stammered.

Brokenly and imperfectly in the ancient world, did the human word voice the truth, dimmed and clouded in the word of thought. In the Orient, it denied the external glory of the Eternal Word speaking in the visible universe. It divided the visible work from the invisible power of the Eternal Word. It denied the divine power of the Eternal Word in creation. It made the various beauty of the universe a phantasmagoria of evil. Here man would utter the incommunicable name, not after the manner in which it was given to man to utter it in the infinite variety of the human word, but even as the Incommunicable uttered Himself in the Eternal Word; and the Orient, daring to scale the infinite height of divine speech, fell into the abyss of nothingness. The Orient named the Incommunicable Nirvana. Therefore in the Orient, the human word possesses no style; it has no power of variety. In Oriental thought there is no image of the external glory of the Eternal Word; in the Oriental word is no expression of the various beauty of the visible universe, proclaiming the glory of its Creator. The

human word in the Orient losés itself in the
symbol and the hieroglyph.

Greece saw the infinite variety of the
visible universe and lived in it. All nature
spoke beauty to the Greek. The glory of
the external universe shone with iridescent
splendor in upon the Greek mind; the
radiant image of the external glory of the
Eternal Word filled Greek thought with its
varied light, and the Greek word gave utterance to the various beauty of the visible
universe in a splendid variety. The Greek
word possesses a style; it has the power of
variety. But the Greek style is purely human; it is limited; it does not rise to sublimity. While Greece saw the visible glory
of creation, it failed to see that it was a
created glory; it failed to recognize it as an
external manifestation of the glory of the
Eternal Word; from the visible things it
rose not to the invisible things of God. Its
accents are always human; it expresses the
various power of the human word, but it
reflects the beauty of the universe without
the knowledge of the power of the Eternal
Word. Therefore did it soon exhaust itself.

It drew its power from the finite life of the creature and died; for the power of the human word only lives, when it draws its virtue from the perennial fullness of the Eternal Word. The human word in Greece in time fell a prey to the rhetorician and to Rome.

Rome knew only the mechanics of the human word. When the Greek rhetorician had reduced the human word to the rule, Rome seized upon the formula and fashioned the human word by the recipe. Rome knew nothing of the Eternal Word, nor did it understand the splendor of the visible universe, but it could borrow the formula from Greece and it understood its mechanical application. It possessed no living style, for style is a living power of the human word; Rome imported the mechanics of style from Greek rhetoricians and produced Cicero.

When the Eternal Word was made flesh, the human word was regenerated; the formless symbolism of the east found the living word, the exhausted variety of Greece was rejuvenated, the dead formula of Rome became instinct with a vigor not its own. Out of the re-created life of mankind blossomed new languages. Christendom, with pentecostal power, spoke many tongues but with the one meaning. From the chaos of the ancient world rose new nations, various, each with a distinct life of its own, a style of its own, but all blossoming from the same trunk, in whose veins circulated the same divine sap, sustaining, nourishing and developing them in the living unity of that one Divine Word made manifest to men in Jesus Christ. Marvelous transformation of the human word made anew by that Uncreate Virtue! The supreme law of art is wonderfully fulfilled. All Christendom speaks a various living tongue, and yet speaks the one word. The confusion of Babel is conquered. Here is unity expressed with a fecund variety and variety sustained by a marvelous unity; unity perpetually unfolding itself in a variety that ever remains various, ever drawing fresh vigor and richer differences from a unity that ever remains one. Though the nations of Christendom speak each its distinct tongue, all speak the same Christianity: the human word, though French in France, is Christian;

though German in Germany, is Christian;
though English in England, Italian in Italy,
Spanish in Spain, various and distinct in
each, with a various beauty of its own in
each, it is in each Christian. The spirit of
the Eternal Word made flesh has breathed
the same power of life into all: the breath
of that life transpires variously in all, has
become the sap of their living structure,
moulding, fashioning, developing, perfecting,
preserving them, beautifying them, organiz-
ing all into one, yet diversifying all into
many. Christendom possesses the fullness
of style—the inexhaustible variety of the
human word—because there has been manifested to it the immeasurable fullness of the
Eternal Word. In this manner does style
unfold itself in the human word of the
nations of Christendom, like many and
various flowers on a single vine. Though
the ancient world spoke many tongues, it
could not diversely utter the same meaning.
Christendom speaks many tongues, but it
ever variously utters the same word of eternal
significance.

We have called style the variety of the

human word. Remembering the supreme
law of art, which we saw to consist in the
expression of unity by variety, we may call
style the art of the human word. Style will
be as various as that word is various. In
that variety lies the freedom of the human
word, and that freedom depends upon its
truth or its correspondence with the word of
thought, and this again depends upon the
truth of things which have their being in the
power of the Eternal Word.

When we touched upon the nature of art
in our third lecture, we traced the genesis
to two factors—the principle of unity and
the manifestation of that unity in variety.
The human intellect, we said, has the power
of apprehending the unity of being in the
visible universe and of expressing that unity
in the word of the mind ; the human imagination has the power of concretely imaging
back the word of thought in a thousand
varying pictures, which may be externally
expressed in manifold shadings and endless
combinations by the spoken word. The
expression of the spoken word is art. Style
is this art, and it resides in this various

power of the spoken word bodying forth the
word of thought by the light and the shade
and the color of the human word. It has
been said that the man is the style. The
manner of utterance makes the style, and the
man is the manner of utterance. The power
of expression is individual because the power
of the imagination is individual, and this
individual power of imagination is as variant
as there are men. Here lies the various
power of the utterance of the word of
thought, here lies the art of the human
word. In this consists the power of that
inexhaustible variety of the human word
which makes style. As the individual imagination diversely catches and pictures the
word of thought, so arise the diversities of
style. Take the same idea and let two men
utter it; one gives a picture full of life and
light, the other a picture dull and leaden.
One opens up splendid vistas of images
glowing and resplendent, the other states his
thought in meagre outline with penurious
precision. The diversity of utterance lies in
the diverse power of the imagination, not in
the truth uttered. In the one, the power of

the imagination is rich and varied, in the other poor and monotonous. As various as are the lineaments of the countenance, so various are the possible diversities of style. No two faces are the same in countless millions, yet all image the one human type.

As in Christendom we discovered diversities of national style, yet all speaking the same Christian word, so in the individuals of any one nation we find many varieties of style, yet all speaking the same national type. It is in the light of the Eternal Word manifested in Jesus Christ that the Christian peoples have conceived the visible universe. The word of thought for them has been supernaturalized and made complete. Each various people speak that supernatural word in its own way, and amongst each people there flourish infinitely various individual expressions of the same supernaturalized word. We have, therefore, the same supernaturalized word of thought common to all Christian peoples, yet diversified by each, and then the various play of innumerable, individual expressions within each living group. The unity of the style of Christendom

is in the supernaturalized word of thought,
like a luminous sun flooding the heaven of
the Christian mind from horizon to horizon.
The variety of this style is the light of that
same word caught and broken and reflected,
first, from the diversified national mind, and
then again caught and broken and reflected
in the various and multitudinous individual
imagination.   Here is a unity expressed in
variety and a variety bounded by unity beyond the power of the thought and the
speech of the ancient world.   The Orient
could not think the Eternal Word because it
refused to think Him in the expression of
His power in the visible universe.   It
dreamed of a formless vastness, therefore
spoke not; it could only symbolize.   Greece
conceived only the fleeting forms of the
external universe, but knew it not as the
visible image of the Eternal Word.   It
blindly spoke that various beauty in the
perishable powers of the human word, unconscious of the roots of its unity in the
Eternal Word.

Rome spoke rhetoric.   It had neither
the inexhaustible variety nor the infinite

unity of the Eternal Word. To Christendom alone has it been given to know the fullness of the variety of that infinite unity; to Christendom alone has been given the fullness of the power of style, for to Christendom alone has been vouchsafed the fullness of the power of the Eternal Word. The human word is in itself limited and perishable, but the supernaturalized human word draws an inexhaustible variety, founded in infinite unity, from the Eternal Word made manifest in the flesh. Christendom ever speaks the same word; but as it is a word whose power is beyond measure and whose variety is inexhaustible, however variously Christendom may speak it can never fully utter that word, never exhaust the infinite possibilities of its manifestation. New peoples may arise to speak that word in ways in which it has never yet been spoken, and yet never begin to utter it adequately. Within each group of new peoples that word may find a manifold variety of new manifestations, and yet there will ever remain an infinite variety possible. Style will be as various as that word is various. In that variety lies the freedom of the human word, the freedom of the human word in the inexhaustible fullness of the truth of the Eternal Word. This freedom of the human word consists in the manner of its utterance, not in what it utters : it *must* utter the true thing. This freedom is only possible when the word of thought is true, and the word of thought is true only when it expresses the truth of the visible universe as founded in the truth of the Eternal Word. Here alone is freedom of speech—the freedom to utter the truth forever and endlessly with all the various powers of the human word charged with the inexhaustible fecundity of the truth of the Eternal Word. The truth alone makes the human word free. In the Orient it was enslaved by the symbol; in Greece its liberty was bounded by the impassable barriers of Fate ; at Rome it was yoked to the dead formula. In Christendom it escapes the symbol in the reality of the Word manifest in the flesh, shatters the bars of Fate by the living truth and bursts the fetters of the formula by the living law.

To speak truth is the sole function of

the human word ; to speak that truth variously, the compass of its freedom. Not to speak truth is its perversion ; not to speak the living truth, its death. To be true, it must be living, and to be living, it must be organic. Rome spoke by the formula and it spoke neither truth nor life. The human word can never utter itself truthfully nor freely by rule. Rhetoric* can not make the human word ; it can only give us its anatomy, its image in death. The rhetorician deals in the word for the word's sake ; but the external word has no true uses save as the outward manifestation of the interior word of life. The external word should be the coin of thought and bear the royal image of the mintage of truth. The rhetorician would have us speak not what we think, but what we feign to think. Talleyrand pronounced the satanic dogma when he said that words were given to hide our thoughts. Feign your speech ; under an artifice of words conceal your thought ; say not what you think, but what

---

* Rhetoric is here used in the sense of artifice in speech, the external patching on of figure and ornament by the application of rules to writing.

you would have others suppose you think.
Say nothing; think nothing; hope nothing;
believe nothing, for in truth, or rather in
parody of truth, there is nothing to think,
to hope, to believe. Define nothing, for
our knowledge is ignorance. The word of
thought is not the image of life; rather
abstract symbol of death. Words, after all,
are but the shadows of nothing. Let us
cover this abyss of emptiness with the artificial flowers of speech. It is not meet for us
to gaze upon it. We must mask Fate, even
as the Greeks did. So speaks the rhetorician. When truth and hope and faith and
life have fled, the rhetorician substitutes the
formula of speech in the endeavor to conceal
the image of death that has crept into their
place. When the life of a people has fled,
its language ceases to live, and then the
rhetorician comes with his formula—his
recipe for style. But he can give no style.
He is a word-broker, dealing in vain forms.
He holds only the empty chrysalis in his
aged hands; the spirit of life has fled.
Style is living; it is not made by rhetoricians or others. It grows by a living law of

the living truth; it springs from a soil
instinct with the life of truth; it draws its
sustenance from the fecundity of the interior
word founded in the image of truth. Its
being is nourished by the heat and light of
truth. It grows from a seed, and like the
seed, it must be planted and cared for and
cultivated. It must be cultivated like a
living thing, not constructed like an artificial thing. The rhetorician would construct
it; therein lies his folly. Cultivation, not
construction, brings the power of the living
word to maturity. Cultivation is toil, painful, long, wearisome, unremitting. Style,
though not made, is formed and fashioned
painfully by an interior power of life. Nature's workshop is a house of labor. Her
processes in making a single flower reach to
the furthest limits of the universe. Note,
too, that she grows her flowers; she does not
manufacture them. Growth comes from
power within, building the living organism
outward. Interior power takes matter from
without to fashion to its own form, to endow
with its own life, making its own image.
The image of the interior word is truth. The

elements of the external word must be organically moulded to that image.

The rhetorician tells us to fashion our style upon some good model. Impotent rule, impossible achievement! How may we be other than ourselves? What value to be a weak copy of a great master? The man is the style. It is his individuality that is his style, and we can no more model our style, save in vapid imitation, upon another's than we can take the fashion and form of another's bodily features. We are ourselves, or nothing. Our style is our own or nothing. But the great master may serve us in cultivating our style, not as a model, which we copy, but as a living word whose power we may assimilate and make our own. The interior power of life, which expresses itself in growth, does not fashion itself to the image of that which it seeks to assimilate. The rose does not make itself into sunlight, but, drinking the vivifying splendor into its own being, gives it forth in the fashion of its own sweet nature, in color and in perfume. Dwell always in the splendor of the noblest speech of the noblest masters, whose speech is noblest because their thought is noblest. Bask in the sunlight of their style until your whole being glows with its fructifying heat, and if the soil of your own thought be good, well-cultivated, then will you speak nobly after your own fashion : You will possess a style. But think not that style is gained by mere absorption. It is not the visible imprint of another's fashion on your own power. No, it is your own activity exercised in self-expression. It is the exploitation of your own personality in the external word. It is the word of thought brought to birth by travail ; it issues forth in visible form only after much labor—the living embodiment of the splendor of truth.

In the various degrees and in the various manners in which truth is apprehended and reflected in the individual mind, so will be the degrees of variety of style. There are, generally speaking, three characteristic styles in the human word.* First, the style of childhood, for the child sees and wonders and admires and expresses his wonder and his admiration. Color and

---

* See Hello's "L'Homme," Part III., L'Art, Le Style.

sound and action are the wonderful pano-
rama of the universe. He sees no more; he
inquires no further. The glitter and the
motion of things take his eye and his imagination. He loves to dwell upon these.
They delight his soul and fill it with a
simple wonder. He details them at length,
repeats and varies his description, but his
variety is limited. He always has the same
epithet for the same thing. This is the style
of Homer. Achilles is always the swift-
footed. The warrior's fleetness of foot has,
once for all, caught the eye and the imagination of the child, and Achilles, under all
circumstances, is ever after the fleet-footed.
Jupiter is always the wise, though over-
reached and duped; Juno always the ox-
eyed, though petulant and jealous; the sea
ever the loud-sounding, though calm and
serene. Here is the human word expressing
the appearance of things in one striking and
fixed phase. The lines of this picture are
serene and simple, its color natural and
striking, but without depth, giving surface
only, unconscious of the power of significance
beneath the gleam of gold or the noise of waters.

The second style is that of the man who has outgrown his childhood. The open-eyed simplicity which fed upon the joyous wonder of the visible universe, caring only to see and tell what it saw, has become the conscious power of observation in the man. He knows that he sees and knows of his power to tell what he sees. Aware of the power of his own word, he turns upon himself and dwells upon that power. Yes, he can utter his thought; he can vary that utterance; he has learned of the wonders of the powers of his speech, and he begins to speak simply for the sake of utterance. He observes nature that she may contribute to the power of his word. Childhood speaks that out of sheer delight it may tell of the wonders of the visible world about it. The man speaks that the visible world may seem to show forth the wonders of his word; Virgil composes the Æneid; we have the age of the artifice of the human word, the age of construction, the day of literary composition, when style is made on models. Virgil admires Homer's style and imitates it. The man of the world would be as simple as the child without the

simplicity of the child, and becomes not simple, but artificial. The fleet-footed Achilles
is a living reality, at whose swiftness of foot
we stand in admiration. Pious Æneas is
a marionette constructed by an artificial
recipe to testify the Roman respect for the
dead formula. Æneas is pious that Rome
may have a patriotic model.

The third style is that of the matured
man, who, indeed, knows the power of the
human word, but knows that power to be
virtuous only in the manifestation of the
living truth. Here style is the conscious
expression of a living power. The matured
man who knows the truth of things and
understands the power of the word in truth,
uses the human word in conscious union
with that truth. He understands with full
knowledge that the human word is for the
purpose of consciously giving manifestation
to the glory of the truth. He uses the word
for truth's sake, never the truth for the
word's sake, never the word for its own
sake. He weighs and tests the value of
words, for he is an artist whose material
must be of the purest and the soundest. He

seeks the fitting word, for the fitting word alone is the true word, and it is the truth of the word which is the test of fitness. The fitness of the word becomes its beauty. Here is the fullness of style, the perfection of style, the style that lives by the power of truth and blossoms from the life of truth. It is the organic style, the style of him who lives in the truth, knows the truth and utters the truth ; and Dante writes the "Divina Comedia."

As the visible universe is the external expression of the power of the Eternal Word, so is the human word the external expression of the power of the interior word of human thought. As the visible universe is the art of the Eternal Word, so is the human word the art of the interior word of thought. Style is the various art of the human word. It is governed by the law of all arts. It is founded in unity expressed by variety. The unity of style is truth, its variety, the individual manner of expressing that truth. The heart of its being is truth. Truth will find expression for itself ; it will find visible utterance, and that utterance various. The human intellect apprehends the unity of the truth of the visible universe; the human imagination receives the white light of truth and breaks it into a thousand varied hues. The human word expresses it in the colors of the human imagination, each individual after his own fashion; though manifold the fashion, the truth is one. Give the same idea to a multitude of minds and it will be reflected in multitudinously various ways; the idea is common to all, the difference lies in the manner of expressing it. What is our own is our style; what is the common property of all is the idea; the man, as we have stated, is the style. Herein lies the difference between genius and mediocrity. Mediocrity will utter the idea in the language of the commonplace; it may rise to the pleasing, it may even violently imitate genius by the *bizarre* and the unusual, but it never ascends to the sublime where genius alone dwells. Genius speaks as the eagle sees—from the mountain top. Its utterance is either in the serenity of the empyrean or in the lurid flash of the swift thunderbolt. The truth it utters is the truth common to all men, but it is the utterance that is uncommon. It is truth spoken from the heights, charged with the irradiant splendor of that loftier atmosphere. It is the human word opening a glimpse into the heavens themselves. It is the same truth which mediocrity utters, but that same truth in the human word transfigured with celestial glory. It is this glory of the human word that constitutes the habitat of genius. By such excess of light mediocrity is blinded. Its weak eye can not gaze upon that splendor. It is given to Moses alone to endure the consuming fires of Sinai. The glory of Mount Tabor is not revealed to the dwellers in the valleys.

The man, we have said, is the style. We now add that, though style depends upon the strain of truth through the individual imagination, the deeper one lives in the truth the loftier and fuller will be his style. It is not enough to know the truth ; one must abide in the truth and the truth in him, for truth is life indeed. The deeper one dwells in the truth and the profounder the indwelling of the truth in him the

sublimer and the profounder ~~in him will~~
be the power of the variety of the human
word.

The truth shall make you free, for truth
is the fullness of life and the fullness of
life is freedom. Style is the freedom of
the human word. The power of its freedom
will be as the power of the truth which it
is the function of the human word to manifest.

The law which governs that manifestation
is the law which governs the being of the
thing manifested ; that supreme law is truth,
for truth is the law of the human word,
the law of the interior word and the law
of life. Truth can not be divided ; it can
not be divorced from its own unity. There
can not be one law for living, another for
thinking and a third for speaking ; there is
but one supreme eternal law, one and the
same, an indivisible power of universal
government : truth in deed, truth in thought
and truth in word. The living law of right-
doing and right-thinking and right-speaking
is truth ; and this is the law of style : to
live the truth, to think as we live and to

speak as we think.* Who lives the truth,
will think the truth, and who lives and
thinks the truth, will speak it. The fuller
and deeper his life in truth the completer
and sublimer his thought of truth, and
the completer and sublimer his thought,
the wider and loftier his expression of
truth by the exalted power of the human
word.

The ancient world had divided the truth
and understood not the unity of this supreme law of style. The Orient sought the
eternal life apart from the visible expression
of the Eternal Word in the order of creation.
It forgot the human deed and the human
word and so petrified in a dream. Greece
sought truth in the human word apart from
the invisible truth of the Eternal Word and
fell exhausted by the wayside. Rome divorced the human word both from the Eternal Word and from the word of thought and

---

* "Il est clair encore que la parole de l'homme doit être con-
forme à la même vérité que sa pensée et son acte, puisqu'il n'y a
pas trois vérités contradictoires. Ainsi l'homme doit: Vivre dans
la vérité; penser comme il vit; et parler comme il pense. Voilà
la loi du style. Nous sommes ici en pleine simplicité, par ce que
nous sommes en pleine vérité."—Hello, "L'Homme," Part III., Le
Style.

made it an artifice.   Christendom alone possesses the unitive fullness of the law.   Truth
in the word by virtue of truth in things;
truth in the visible universe by the power
of the Eternal Word, Who is the Eternal
Truth of the Eternal Life.